Tove Stang Dahl

Women's Law

Tove Stang Dahl

Women's Law
An Introduction to Feminist Jurisprudence

Translated by Ronald L. Craig

Norwegian
University Press

Norwegian University Press (Universitetsforlaget AS), 0608 Oslo 6
Distributed world-wide excluding Scandinavia by
Oxford University Press, Walton Street, Oxford OX2 6DP

London   New York   Toronto
Delhi   Bombay   Calcutta   Madras   Karachi
Kuala Lumpur   Singapore   Hong Kong   Tokyo
Nairobi   Dar es Salaam   Cape Town
Melbourne   Auckland

and associated companies in
Beirut   Berlin   Ibadan   Mexico City   Nicosia

© Universitetsforlaget AS 1987
Reprinted 1988

ISBN 82-00-18490-0

British Library Cataloguing in Publication Data
Dahl, Tove Strang
Women's law: an introduction to feminist jurisprudence.—(Scandinavian library)
1. Women—Legal status, laws, etc.
I. Title II. Series
342.2'878   K644

Printed in Denmark
by P. J. Schmidt A/S, Vojens

Contents

Preface

The subject of *women's law* was recognized as an autonomous legal discipline by the Faculty of Law, University of Oslo, in 1974. The first students arrived in 1975; since then teaching and research have been going on regularly, from 1978 at the *Institute of Women's Law* in the Department of Public Law. To our knowledge, the Oslo Faculty thus pioneered the subject of women's law and gave it facilities for development that are not at all common at Western universities.

In 1985 members of our Institute published a two-volume collection of our main writings through the years, *Kvinnerett I-II*, from which the publisher requested me to collect my own contributions for a separate publication in English.

In preparing this particular volume I have enjoyed the inspiring assistance of many friends and colleagues—above all from Helga Maria Hernes, editor of the series in which the Norwegian version was originally included, and from Ronald L. Craig, J.D., who undertook the task of translating the text, and with whom I consequently have had many interesting discussions on the differences between our native legal systems.

Several others have contributed to the English edition: Maureen Cain, Jon Elster, and Gunvor Nyquist all made great efforts to clarify my arguments as well as my prose. Kristin Robberstad and Elisabeth Sletten of the staff of our Institute typed the script with their usual accuracy. For their previous assistance, I am grateful to Harriet Holter, who included an earlier version of chapter 6 in her anthology *Patriarchy in a Welfare Society* (Oslo: Universitetsforlaget 1984), and to the *International Journal of the Sociology of Law*, which in 1982 and 1984 published pieces similar to those appearing here as chapters 6 and 7.

For their generous grants to the publication I am also grateful to the two Norwegian research councils, NAVF and NORAS.

Oslo, at the Institute of Women's Law

June 1987

Tove Stang Dahl

Part One
Introducing Women's Law

1

Why Women's Law?

1.1. The Purpose of Women's Law

To be a woman is a personal attribute to which only a few rules attach legal significance according to Norwegian law. Legislation is wholly gender-neutral, and the aim is that it shall be as gender-neutral as possible. Consequently, the remnants of formal sex discrimination from earlier times have essentially been eradicated in the course of the last 15 years. Soon it will only be the Constitution's prescription of agnatic succession to the Norwegian Crown which remains, i.e., that 'only male born in lawful wedlock may succeed male' (Article 6, paragraph 1). The gender-neutral imprint is corroborated by the Equal Status Act,[1] which prohibits different treatment of women and men in almost all aspects of society, but which is especially aimed at improving the position of women (Equal Status Act, sections 1–3).

A further explanation is necessary for the seemingly peculiar situation that women's law should happen to originate and develop as a legal discipline at the same time as sex discrimination in the body of law is either being whittled down or completely abolished. The explanation lies both in the structure of law and in women's increasing opportunities. Just as the French revolution resulted in the introduction of equality under the law, thus prohibiting both the poor and the rich from sleeping under the bridge, equality under the law today does not preclude the practice of discrimination. Rules on equality of treatment do not, of themselves, materialize into equal or just results, either in individual cases or collectively. Often it is

---

1. In addition to ensuring substantive equality of treatment between the sexes, the Act is also intended to influence attitudes towards sex roles. The Act established the position of the Equal Status Ombudsman and the Equal Status Appeals Board.

just the opposite, that the goal of equality demands unequal treatment in order to give weak parties or groups the opportunity for equality and equal worth. In this respect law can only be properly evaluated if one, in addition to understanding the text of the law and its intention, has insight into the law's consequences for individuals.

As long as we live in a society where men and women have different paths in life, different living conditions, with different needs and opportunities, legal rules will necessarily affect men and women differently. And silence strengthens inequality and injustice, regardless of the legislators' intentions. It is this complex interplay between law and life that researchers in women's law seek to chart and understand, with the special goal of contributing to the work for real equality and liberation. The possibility of achieving this is today realistic with the entry of women into universities, as teachers, researchers and students, and with the universities' openness to the new direction of critically oriented disciplines.

Feminist Perspective of the Law
The following description of women's law will stretch beyond what is usually considered legal theory. For a good solid legal analysis one is usually expected to apply the same thought process, the same definition of legal issues, and the same method for solving them, as those who originally produced the rules or those who later presumably apply them (see section 2.2). As with the study of women's law in other countries, the objective here is to apply a systematic feminist perspective as well, i.e., to examine and understand how women are considered in law and how the law corresponds to women's reality and needs (Atkins and Hoggett 1984:1).

For some it may seem one-sided to apply a specific group's perspective and needs. But upon closer examination one may observe how it is the law itself which is one-sidedly based. It is still today the man's norm that applies in most areas, so that it is for the most part the opinions, needs and conflicts of men which are codified in law. This norm also contains a statement of how women are or ought to be. Most parts of this book will give examples of this.

The fact that law reflects both men's and women's reality from a man's point of view does not mean that there exists a conspiracy of men furthering this purpose. If such were the case, it would be difficult to explain progress over the last 150 years regarding the legal status of women both in Norway and many other places in the world. Nevertheless men continue to sit in the most important positions. Law is an important part of the cultural hegemony that men have in our type of society, and a cultural hegemony means that a ruling group's special way of viewing social reality is accepted as normal and as a part of the natural order of things, even by those who are in fact subordinated by it. In this way law contributes to maintaining the ruling group's position.

A renowned American feminist expresses it by saying that 'sex class' is so deep that it is invisible (Firestone 1970). The differences comprise in reality almost every aspect of our lives, and are so pervasive that one often fails to notice them. Men and women dress differently, occupy themselves differently, have different activities in the market, in the family and in public life, use leisure time differently, have different social ties and different sexualities. The differences in themselves are not, however, the problem. The problem is how they are mutually ranked, and that in society's evaluations of the sexes, women's qualities, characteristics, values and activities are systematically subordinated to men's (Jaggar 1983:85).

As a result of this ranking women often emerge as either something other than or 'less' than men. In her account of classical liberal political philosophy Helga Hernes describes how women are often considered 'mini-persons': 'They have little moral aptitude, little intellect, little right to property, and equality within certain limits. But man has more of everything and therefore also position and authority' (Hernes 1982a:17). Hume, Hobbes, Locke, Rousseau and Hegel all attached question marks to women's status as persons, both in terms of moral philosophy and law. Women's present under-representation in important political institutions and professions can be explained as a natural consequence of the past perception of women, just as much as it can be by past discriminatory policies, which meant that women were consciously and systematically excluded from the professions in public life (Ibid:13).

Today women are on the way in. But law is an arena where change is often slow in coming. Law as an institution to a large degree contributes to the maintenance of the traditional male hegemony in society. At the same time law is fertile soil for the cultivation of rules which can provide a foundation for vast changes, including the relationship between the two sexes. If the position of women is to be improved, this must also be done through the law, and this is acknowledged by today's lawmakers. Insight into the structure and effect of legal rules is therefore necessary for such comprehensive changes as will be discussed here.

A special problem arises when legislation in certain situations 'runs ahead' of the development in society, and in this way creates an idealistic gap between the factual reality in society and the legal rule. Modern legislation on sexual equality, and the general gender-neutralization of the body of law illustrates this. Law can presume a likeness which does not exist in reality, and which thus results in unforeseen or even unintended consequences with regard to the situation of women. In many areas of working life the powerlessness of the Equal Status Ombudsman in the face of obvious breaches of the Equal Status Act becomes in itself detrimental to the development of a general public notion of justice in the area of equal rights (Halvorsen 1985 a and b). The new Children Act (Law on Children and Parents of 8 April 1981, No. 1) can also in some respects be considered a law of 'false' equality, in that it operates according to its aim only in a society where there is in fact parity between the mother and father regarding time shared with and care of children, parity among children born in and out of wedlock, and parity among fathers who are married to the child's mother and those who aren't. Such an idealistic equality creates both legally technical and practical problems, such as, for example, the repeal of the preference given to the mother in child custody cases. The repeal of this preference after the breakdown of a relationship has not merely weakened the position of women, but also created a series of new conflicts between parents, who can no longer adapt themselves to the predictability of applicable law, a situation which is most likely not in the 'child's best interest', as the lawmakers had intended.

In addition to examining existing law from a feminist perspective, it is an important task of women's law to examine whether new areas and issues ought to be brought out of judicial voids and subjected to the scrutiny of the law. This concerns especially issues about work and caretaking within the sphere of our private lives, issues about sexuality and emotional life. Making such issues legal issues could have several consequences beyond the immediate improvement of women's position. Among other things it would upset the relationship between family and state and contribute to making the distinction between the private and public sphere different from what it is today.

The State and Women
The state has become progressively more important for women, both in the mobilization and integration of women as participants in the political system, and in the expansion of state duties. Up to now and even today our form of state, in both its aspects of the rule of law and the welfare state, can to a large extent be considered a guardian state for women, since women themselves have only to a limited extent participated in its distribution of benefits and evils. Women have had a marginal role in the administration of such things and in the relevant organizations, and have also been indirect rather than direct recipients of redistribution. This, of course, is a consequence of women's weak position in the market and firm anchorage in the family (Hernes 1982b:29, Ketscher 1984:28). Women have, in other words, to a far greater extent than men, been subjected to state paternalism regarding protective legislation and have thereby also been subjected to the social control which the state has established in these areas. The question thus becomes whether women's greater participation can possibly change the situation through the promotion and incorporation of women's own interests in legislation and administration.

The development of the public social security system has transferred—or rather given back—large resources to women. But women's client status within the social security system is in many cases different, weaker and more controlled than men's, many examples of which will be given in this book.

With respect to the market there have also been changes in women's responsibility and workload since World War II. The work of women has to a large degree become professionalized and publicly oriented, and in Norway this has happened through state administration and the development of the public health and social welfare sector. This development has transformed the private spheres of women's work to public service, from unpaid housework to paid work with the state administration as employer. This 're-zoning of the family into a public entity' (Hernes 1982 b) has given women a greater dependence upon the state, for better and for worse. The development has given women money and work outside the home, but has also subjected larger areas of caretaking to administrative and bureaucratic control.

An important question is to what extent such an administrative transfer of responsibility and professionalization has a tendency to de-humanize care, and thus society. An examination of the development that has taken place in the nursing sector would reveal that the care for the sick and needy can easily be found wanting with high-technology treatment and aid, and that the professionalization of nursing leads to a loss in overall ability to provide needed care and assistance (Martinsen and Wærness 1979). The problem concerns large parts of the modern health and social service system, where division of work, specialization and efficiency characterize the nature of care, in stark contrast to the organization and values of the local milieu. In the end, paid work in the public sector will probably be characterized by the same alienating mechanisms that have marked paid work in the private sector, despite the fact that women's work in the public sector to a large degree consists of service and client work and not the production of goods.

As women's participation in the state increases, both as politicians, clients and paid workers, the rationale for the extensive gender-based paternalism will probably weaken. The general paternalism is, however, a structural phenomenon of the welfare state, and will probably always be debated (Dahl 1983). The question of whether and to what extent women want and ought to make use of the state remains.

The Norwegian women's movement in general, and thereunder Norwegian women researchers, have in many ways been more 'state friendly' than in other countries. It is probably related to the opportunities we in the Scandinavian welfare states have for utilizing the law as an instrument for social change. 'State optimists' in feminist politics have acted out of a conviction that weak parties and groups must make use of intercessors as coordinating centres to strengthen their positions. Such a conviction should not, however, preclude scepticism to increased state intervention as a useful mechanism; and in any case its usefulness is to be evaluated from case to case and over time. Whether, to what extent, and in what ways these questions can and ought to be made legal issues create both methodological and jurisprudential challenges. The making of these questions into legal issues also has its price, in terms of both the relationship between individuals and the relationship between the individual and the state (Sverdrup 1984a, Hellum 1985, Fastvold 1985, Ketscher 1984, Eriksson 1985).

Given this background, the purpose of women's law is to describe, explain and understand the legal position of women, with the specific aim of improving the position of women in law and in society.

1.2. Feminism and Research

Women's law as a discipline belongs to two social science traditions: the established legal science and the young discipline of women studies, which has been accepted in many academic areas at universities in many countries during the 1970s and 1980s. Here I will give a perspective of women's law as specially related to women studies, while chapters 2–5 will deal specifically with women's law as a legal discipline.

Feminism

As women studies, women's law is a part of the new feminist movement with its origin in the USA from the middle of the 1960s. Feminist movements have been a part of history, at any rate during the two last centuries, but never before had they assumed the breadth and depth of the new modern feminism. The word 'feminism' originated in French politics in the nineteenth century as a description of different groups that in one way or another sought to improve the position of women. During the twentieth century the concept has at times been reserved for women politicians who have emphasized how women are different from men, i.e., women's special qualities, women's unique nature, motherhood's mystic experiences, and women's special purity. These tendencies in feminist politics have been characterized as 'sex romantic' and are largely replaced by more 'sex rationalistic' political movements (Jaggar 1983:5). Both liberal and marxist feminism can be characterized as 'sex rationalistic'.

Rather than emphasize differences, they emphasize the similarities between women and men. The liberals maintain that women's weak position is due to society's irrationality—not because women are different (or better) than men, but because in reality there exists a fundamental similarity between the sexes that society overlooks, to its own detriment in terms of loss of resources and impracticable arrangements. The marxists consider capitalism the fundamentally oppressive system for both women and men, who in reality are the same, but become different as a result of 'the dual oppression' women are subjected to. That is, in addition to the general oppression, which also affects men, women are particularly oppressed by the sex-divided labour market, which utilizes women as cheap labour and reserve labour, without consideration for women's social needs for special rights in connection with pregnancy and birth.

Even if we accept that feminism has historically assumed various forms and has contained extremely different philosophies and ideologies, it is in my opinion appropriate to apply the concept broadly—as a description of all the movements and women's groups that, for different reasons in one way or another, strive to work against the oppression of women and in general for the improvement of the position of women.

However, this good intention is not always best served by the ideological underpinnings of the different groups. Within liberal feminism equality with men occupies, and rightly so, a central position in the traditional view that all people are equal, being grounded on the objective of justice and equality for all citizens. In earlier times this worked well. Liberal women and men stood together in demanding the same formal rights for women as for men. John Stuart Mill, in opposition to classical scholars in liberal political philosophy, was one of the foremost spokesmen for women's equal rights in the nineteenth century, and his opinions were broadly applied during the struggle for women's rights around the turn of the century. In Norway too liberal men from both the Conservative Party and the Liberal Party preached the cause of women, particularly in the fight for the right to vote. However, new problems arose when women began to abandon the goal of formal (de jure) equality for a strategy demanding real (de facto) equality, as was demanded during the 1970s. With the demand for quotas and positive discrimination for women in order to achieve de facto equality, many women lost touch with the liberal ideology of equal treatment. We began to perceive the features of this split during the debate prior to the enactment of the Equal Status Act. And it has later been widened in that more and more groups of women now demand greater utilization of positive discrimination.

Marxist feminists have also incurred problems, because the marxist tradition only addresses parts of women's lives. Through the one-sided emphasis on paid work as the organizing institution in community life, marxist ideology lost the element of a feminist perspective, and today there hardly exists any distinctive marxist feminist politics. Also among feminists who consider themselves socialists, it is unclear where the loyalty to traditional socialist approach (industrial organization, trade union etc.) ends and the feminist ideology takes over.

All directions of feminist politics share the same ideals: equality, justice and freedom. But they have different opinions about what is unequal, unjust and oppressive [see chapter 5 for further details]. There is also disagreement about where the shoe pinches most, and about what can and ought to be done. The different theoretical frameworks and the basic values they build upon also give different descriptions of reality. But through all the different descriptions a new reality emerges when the feminist perspective is applied. It is at this point that feminist theory can unite the different directions within general political theory and philosophy. Feminism crosses both liberal/marxist ideology and non-socialist/socialist politics, while individual feminist issues even supplement each of the conflicting ideologies and groupings.

We also see this unifying feminist perspective in women studies. Though based on different politico-philosophical foundations, women studies to a large extent address a series of common themes. New areas such as sexuality, birth, emotional life and caretaking are drawn into the treatment of analytical research. Women studies explore women's work (which is far more than paid work and other work in the economic market), women's use of time, and a series of other differences in the lives and living conditions of the sexes.

Women's law, with its feminist foundation, also brings new areas and questions in under juridical treatment. It has been an important task to apply to existing law a feminist perspective that crosses the individual disciplines, be they family law, social security law, criminal law or labour law. Furthermore, to create new concepts for the gathering of legal issues within 'birth law',[2] 'housewives' law',[3] 'paid-work law',[4] and 'money law'.[5] All these concepts have originated and been applied on the basis of the distinct priority that a feminist perspective of law must necessarily entail: (1) a description and evaluation of existing law; (2) an identification of areas of strong legal support, weak legal support, and judicial voids where 'legal' issues have not even been addressed; and (3) discussion of whether and how the body of law ought to be expanded, contracted or replaced.

Knowledge and Interests
The origin of our knowledge lies in our individual and collective experiences. These experiences are moulded out of the reality we live in everyday. But through reflection and toil our reality is also fashioned by our experiences. Through this interplay between reality's influence on humans and human temperament and human temperament's influence on reality, there are created different opinions of the same reality. Thus, women's and men's description and opinions of reality can be extremely different.

2. 'Birth law' is the gathering, systematization, and analysis of many fragmented legal rules that specifically concern the creation and planning of newborn life.
3. 'Housewives law' gathers, systematizes and analyzes legal rules on the care of households and family and all that concerns women as part-time, overtime or full-time housewives. See chapter 7.
4. The term 'paid work' is used throughout the book to emphasize the fact that women do an enormous amount of work for which they are not paid. 'Paid-work law' thus, examines the unjust legal position of women in the marketplace.
5. 'Money law' addresses legal rules concerning the distribution of money in society.

The two sexes simply live different lives, experience different things, and of course have different perceptions of the reality surrounding them, of what is conspicuous and important or of what is obscure and marginal. Feminist philosophy and research involve a constant re-writing of reality through the fresh identification of particularly urgent questions needing investigation. This 'reconstruction' of reality (Jaggar 1983:381) emphasizes aspects of human lives and living conditions other than those men emphasize.

An uncomfortable feeling that the situation seems unjust when one compares the conditions of women and men, and repeated personal experiences that reinforce the same feeling—such unsystematic experiences help to create the opinion that women are oppressed, and that the oppression is due to society's assessment of the differences between the two sexes. These more or less obscure and unconnected observations and opinions lead one to investigate either the negative sides of society or of the law. It is through criticism that wrongs are described and explained; it is through awareness and understanding of these wrongs that conditions are created to counteract them. This is one side of what we often call critical awareness. However, one does not speak only of 'negative' awareness. If one wants social change one must also identify desired conditions and visions. Thus, there is also talk of 'positive' awareness.

The lives and situations of women also involve positive experiences. Even if feminine culture in many ways is a reflection of the ruling male culture via patriarchy, sub-cultures have their own positive and renewing qualities that women researchers are helping to make people aware of (Haukaa 1977).

One of the objectives of women studies is to reveal the form and content of alternative women's culture. On the one hand, it bears the imprint of patriarchy's cultural hegemony—with a feminine culture as a result—on the other hand, something else has been created out of the experiences and strengths of women. We must continue to build upon it and to extend it into the culture of men. This search for elements in an alternative culture, by finding and developing a positive women's culture, is an objective of women studies.

Women's law contributes to this by identifying women-centred policy considerations to be applied in law. Such policy considerations fall into two categories—the ideal and the political. The former concerns the identification of certain basic values and their crystallization; the latter concerns the areas to which we want to give political priority. Juridically, the establishment of such policy considerations provides guidelines for the organization of legal material, for evaluating and changing the law, and also to some extent for the interpretation of rules and application of law—on a par with other policy considerations as they are accorded weight as sources of law. Politically, we mean the basic values upon which we want to build our visions and priorities and thereby our strategies promoting women's interests. To apply a feminist perspective to legal rules means therefore that one perceives legal rules in the light of both women's experiences and interests (for a more detailed account of this see chapter 5).

Women studies have devoted much energy to the nature and means of oppression of women. As a result more and more unreasonable disparities between women and men, and among women themselves, have been described and explained. In this way women studies have until now to a large extent consisted of studies of misery. This has also been the case with women's law. Extreme differences between women and men's rights have, for example, been revealed in social security law and paid-work law. We have also been concerned with how women are victims of male violence and sexual coercion. The more examples that are gathered, the greater the possibility to see them in a proper context.

Here we come to the next step in a scientific process: the search for understanding. To understand the legal situation of women is the epistemological goal of women's law. Understanding means finding the connections, seeing totalities. Description and explanation can be fragmented. To understand is to reflect on the connections, for example, to find several connections between the same phenomena, to formulate them as explicitly and precisely as possible (Føllesdal et al. 1983:56 f). The theory of 'the tripartite support system' for women and 'the two-track support system' for men is by way of example a theory of gender-specific connection between the individual's status in money law *and* their main sources of income. It is a theory of a complicated whole whose mutual connections are grounded and made explicit (the theory is explained in more detail in chapter 6).

1.3. Science and Politics

I have attempted to describe essential phases and elements in a research process. All of our insights to begin with are tentative and hypothetical. We group and use experiences, intuition, reflection; we use these sources of knowledge to describe and understand fragments of reality. From this we fashion new ideas and hypotheses of how things are, and maybe how they hang together. Gradually the connections appear, increasing our understanding. Our hypotheses become more nuanced, better grounded, and give a basis for a more systematic examination and more opportunity to perceive additional connections with a keener understanding and greater capability to treat the subject.

In women studies we emphasize our place in the politically oriented women's movement. It was natural and necessary when we began our work—brought together with widespread different experiences, half-baked slogans and incoherent convictions. All the proposed definitions of women's law in the first years naturally contained a political element. Today the bonds with the women's movement are still strong. But there are more reasons to discuss the differences between the women's movement and women studies. While politics first and foremost deals with power—i.e. the distribution of benefits and evils, questions of participation, joint decision-making and self-determination—it is the primary duty of science to seek knowledge and understanding, and by means of this to promote action. The women's movement is often—for many good reasons—forced to make strategic decisions and to simplify facts that women researchers cannot always agree with. Problems can arise, especially when we are of the opinion that our position based on the findings of our research would give better results in the long run, whereas the movement needs arguments for short-sighted political advantages.

On the other hand, there will always be an interplay between science and politics, and in women's law we ought, in my opinion, to seek the most active possible interplay between the two. The reasoning and results of research can establish norms and promote action if the research offers insight when situations arise, and contributes to setting new problems on the agenda on its own by teaching, writing and acting. The movement for the provision of centres for battered women, rape victims etc., thus arose amidst such interaction between research and politics. From the very beginning researchers took part, and the movement probably would not have got off the ground so quickly and effectively as it did without the stimulus of insights obtained by researchers on the extent and nature of wife battering and abuse of women generally (Fodstad and Steen 1976, Dahl 1980). The founding of Legal Advice for Women (JURK) in 1974 is an example of a combined effort of research and legal assistance with clear and direct political relevance. Later the organization was converted to an independent legal assistance institution, but with the continued contact and cooperation with women's law (Dahl 1984:37 and Halvorsen 1985 a:45).

Every political theory must have its vision of the good society. It is this vision which will give it the strength to renew itself. In women's law such visions from feminist politics contribute to carrying it beyond mere negative criticism—critical law—and towards a positive construction of another law, a so-called 'alternative jurisprudence'.[6] This alternative jurisprudence ought in my opinion to consist of theory construction, together with proposals and strategies for reform and major change in society. I have much less faith in developing a doctrine of alternative interpretation, such as some critical legal scholars have championed. Such an approach is not only difficult and to a degree impossible to accomplish. It can also carry with it a threat to civil liberties, if such an approach were to have even a temporary breakthrough regarding the application of law. Another point is that an emphasis upon previously unperceived women-centred policy considerations can to some degree be presumed to have influence upon the application of traditional sources of law (see chapter 4 for further details).

---

6. With his article 'Draft for a Marxist Jurisprudence' Lars D. Eriksson has initiated an intense and varied Nordic discussion on the possibilities of developing an alternative jurisprudence and use of legal strategy in political work (see the series of articles, especially in *Retfærd*, Nos. 11, 12, 14, 15, 19, as well as Håkan Hydén's summarization and analysis in *Law as an Instrument for Social Change*, Hydén (ed.) 1982).

With our grounding in criticism we seek to identify unreasonable discrimination and injustice and to provide alternatives that contribute to greater equality. With such grounding in the established order one would seek first a politics of equality to correct inequality, making the unequal more equal. Thereafter, one's work for justice and freedom could lead to the positive goals entailed in the concept 'liberation' and to further discussions of what we call 'women-centred policy considerations' (for further details see chapter 5).

2

Women's Law as Legal Science

Women's law takes as its base women; it describes and evaluates the law from a feminist perspective. The new methods employed are found at several levels.

The feminist perspective establishes a systematic cross-section through existing rules of law in order to perceive otherwise unnoticed connections (see L. Smith 1975) of significance for all individuals, but especially and directly for women. This means that we in women's law attach greater weight to law's systematizing function, and thereunder its concept formation and theory construction, in comparison to what is usual in law.

In addition, the feminist perspective attributes greater substantive content to several sources of law. It directs attention to the consideration of women-relevant aims reflected in the legislative processes; it increases knowledge of both general public opinion of what the law is or ought to be and the actual practice of individuals; and it provides alternative raw materials for a result-oriented application of precedent and for other practice etc. But it is especially the emphasis upon women-centred policy considerations that both broadens the basis of evaluation in the use of policy considerations generally in interpreting law and functions as an independent source of law. The emphasizing of women-centred policy considerations and their basic values also influences the underlying values which help to form the major premises for the harmonizing of legal sources (Aarbakke 1966).

Before I go into more detail, I will state what is found in the person-directed approach and its juridically interdisciplinary consequence.

2.1. A Person-Directed and Juridically Interdisciplinary Discipline

Legal groundings in personality, status and capacity have a long tradition in legal history, as regards both general rights of the individual and the legal status of particular groups, for example, children, the insane, the incompetent, etc. But in modern law the significance of the ideas of personality, status and capacity have declined, being replaced by other approaches. This development was confirmed by the decision taken in 1970 at the University of Oslo to abolish personality, status and capacity as a separate discipline of the study of law. Later it appears, however, that the use of person-directed bases as the technique of attack and an operative perspective has once again become an object of special attention within law. Law has evolved from its historical focus on private property, commerce and the state, to also include people's more everyday problems. The origin of women's law is a part of this development.

Weak groups have found their representatives. Child law is, for example, a person-directed discipline whose objective is the study and improvement of a specific group's legal status. There is talk of immigration law, patient law, law of prisoners' rights, and law of the elderly. Even within classic commercial law, weak parties have opted out of the law of sales and found their place in consumer law. Anita Dahlberg, who heavily emphasizes the person-directed base and its associated interest as a systematizing criterium, points to new titles of books within the above-mentioned areas, adding titles like 'Student law', 'Teacher law', and 'Wage-earner law' (Dahlberg 1981: 148). Similarly Lotta Westerhäll-Gisselsson emphasizes how the person-directed base is essential and 'that which is most characteristic of women's law, that which makes it provocative' (Westerhäll-Gisselsson 1979:11).

When women's law is compared with other person-directed disciplines, there exists similarity both in the application of a person-directed cross-section through rules of law, and in the desire to improve one's own group's status. But while several of the disciplines mentioned are more narrow with respect to the defined group's size and legal character, women's law has a special feature, namely, its very large and complex segment of the population, which in turn has exceedingly many and extremely varied sub-groups. Women's law therefore finds its place within all the other disciplines and constitutes a relative part of them: women are elderly, immigrants, prisoners, patients, etc. This broadens the field of women's law enormously in relation to the other person-directed disciplines. It is not *one* role, *one* interest, *one* function or *one* minority group that women's law serves in the way consumer law is concerned with the consumer, patient law with the patient, etc.

Most of the other person-directed disciplines have defining characteristics codified in formal law that delimit the legal issues that at any rate must be taken up. In child law the statutory age limit of a child and the special protective legislation for children become the natural bases for describing the core area of the discipline. In the law of prisoners' rights there are no delimiting personal or biological qualities, but rather the circumstances which demand that a host of requirements codified in law be met. The person-in-question must be alleged to have committed an act in violation of the Criminal Code. She must be found and charged. She must be either incarcerated pending trial or convicted and sentenced in accordance with the Criminal Code and the Criminal Procedure Act and subjected to punishment in prison, regulated by the Prison Act. The relevant laws here are obvious, first and foremost the Prison Act, which is aimed at the regulation of the life of prisoners. Secondarily, the laws of penal institutions address legal issues that are considered to be significant for prisoners and prison life. It is at this point that the subject becomes juridically interdisciplinary, since the relevant laws all belong to public law, more specifically criminal law.

Women's law has few signposts in formal law. The few that exist are naturally of special interest. That a law is gender-specific in its formulation need not, however, mean that it is significant for women's position in law or society. The same applies to the directives found in sex discrimination legislation. Even though its express objective gives it an automatic relevance to women's law, and even though the act's enforcement measures are many and comprehensive, this in itself is not tantamount to the law's consequences having special significance for women's lives and rights, either generally or in decisions in individual cases. In fact, investigations into the practice surrounding the Equal Status Act reveal in effect no special significance for women. It appears to be particularly difficult to formulate consistently effective sex discrimination legislation (Halvorsen 1985 b and c). Such legislation is nevertheless of interest to women's law. Its study increases understanding of the relationship between law on paper and law in reality, between law and society, and between women and law. Even though sex-discrimination legislation does not work in individual cases in accordance with its objectives, and even though it does not appear to have immediate effect for women as a group, the law and the government authorities enforcing sex-discrimination legislation do make up important aspects of the public debate on sex discrimination. Together with other programs this can contribute in the long run to influencing attitudes in society.

Women's law knows no formal limitations other than the feminist perspective. This means that the discipline crosses the borders between private law and public law and in general the borders between all facets of law. This has its background in the fact that women are defined as women through a whole series of relationships, from the most intimate and private to the most open and public.

Such an all-embracing classification gives little guidance as to how the discipline is to be constructed and what content it should have. Women make up the largest existing population group and are found in all age groups and in most strata of life and society. The subject of women's law is thus not merely juridically interdisciplinary, but comprises in principle all areas of law, the entire legal science. No legal issue, in theory, is without relevance for women's law before it is examined.

The fundamental borderlessness of the cross-section made by women's law means in my opinion that an essential part of the discipline's methodology and theory ought to be aimed at finding its systematic criteria for the circumscription and construction of women's law. Before I go into specifics, it may prove useful to comment upon the more general task of legal systematics.

2.2. Doctrine and Science

Legal doctrine can be considered the core of legal science. The sources of law are its foundation; the theory of sources of law, its methodology.[1] This theory encourages a judicial approach to solving legal problems, in as much as the sources of law used in legal doctrine are the same as those used by judges; and the methodology in legal doctrine is the same as the judges' rules for ranking the sources, for harmonizing or choosing among them when they are in conflict, etc.

Per Augdahl expresses it thus: the one who formulates legal rules often '... considers that which he formulates to be the rules which—all reservations taken into account ...—presently have the best foundation to work as guiding principles for the courts (and other administrative authorities) and are therefore the ones most suitable to be applied' (Augdahl 1973:27).

Legal doctrine and the judge's decision-making process in questions of law are in other words similar methodologically speaking. But the legal scholar has a broader function. Whereas the judge makes a decision in an individual case, the legal scholar should guide both the judge and others who apply the law—administrative civil servants who make decisions in individual cases, who write reports, draft regulations and guidelines, as well as legislators, politicians and others interested in legal science.

The legal scholar should put individual decisions in their proper context, and through this systematizing of positive law, an inner order is established. This, the legal scholar does, using much of the same methodology applied by the judiciary. Anna Christensen emphasizes how legal doctrine 'works' *within* the system; even belongs to the system. The primary task is to bridge the gap between the law's abstract norms and the concrete reality of the law as applied. The abstract contents of norms are operationalized, 'gravitating down' to more concrete levels while the court's concrete decisions 'work their way up', integrating with the abstract contents of norms (Christensen 1984:13).

It is not unusual to equate legal doctrine with legal science,

---

1. 'Legal doctrine or legal analysis is a conceptual practice that combines two characteristics: the willingness to work from the institutionally defined materials of a given collective tradition and the claim to speak authoritatively within this tradition, to elaborate it from within in a way that is meant, at least ultimately, to affect the application of state power' (Unger 1986). The end-product of legal doctrine is a description of law as it is, as opposed to what it ought to be.

especially if one grants legal doctrine a certain flexibility for evaluations of legal politics and ethics and evaluations of the factual groundings of law.[2] In my opinion it is useful to make the distinction. Legal doctrine, i.e., the interpretation of law according to prescribed methodology, should remain the core area of legal science because it is there that lawyers have their own tools and a distinct craft. Legal science—legal theory—embraces, and ought to embrace, more. One characteristic of a theory is that it gives ordered and general statements about certain connections between phenomena. This involves not only connections in the sense of harmony between fragments of rules and sets of rules, but also connections in a broader sense and on other levels, for example, between rules and reality, between rules and various ideologies, etc. Statements of the latter type require new sources, and new methodological bases—I would emphasize particularly the empirical and moral/political bases (see chapters 4 and 5 for further details).

It is not, however, the case that legal doctrine excludes empirical and political bases from its argumentation. On the contrary, many legal scholars expressly state that such factors are to be given weight. And the wider the boundary one is willing to draw around the bases of legal doctrine, the more insignificant the distinction between legal doctrine and legal science becomes. A strict legal positivist will, on the other hand, draw a narrower boundary around the definition of legal doctrine, distinguishing it from both social science, on the one hand, and legal politics, on the other. The more modern, broader definition often gives a rather wide scope to the legal politics factor, and also a certain scope to empiricism. This is at least the case within the 'consequence-oriented' and the 'realistic' legal theory, which is at present heavily emphasized at the Faculty of Law at the University of Oslo.

Even though the need to explain the distinction between legal doctrine and legal science is of less importance the more one enlarges the category of legal doctrine, it is my opinion that it is useful to maintain the distinction. To some degree the comparatively narrow definition of legal doctrine highlights the

---

2. 'Legal politics' is a term rarely used in English. It denotes considerations, not of what the law is, but of what the law ought to be. Legal politics is therefore normative in character.

distinctiveness and essence of its function; to some degree it can serve to emphasize that legal science can—and ought—to be something more: a science that ought to systematically seek out secondary and tertiary bases for its theories, which in turn provide a body of methodological rules which considers factors other than positive sources of law. These rules must, of course, be formulated with great care, paying specific attention to their underpinnings, mutual connections and contrast to legal doctrine. Today some data on reality are usually incorporated, but their use often seems random and at any rate unsystematic. The use of legal political analysis as a part of legal doctrine, however, proves to be more systematic.

If we maintain the distinction between legal doctrine and other tasks of legal science, we preserve a means of illuminating the complexity of legal science's objectives in the gray zone between law's practical and theoretical extremes.

The *practical* interest is well-known and documented, and spans from the general service legal scholars can give those who apply the law, for example, through handbooks and law commentaries, to communicating and simplifying legal material intended for specialists. Such work can increase understanding, making law more useful to new groups and thus of greater practical significance for the welfare of these groups. Women's law as a discipline has, for example, the important task of examining the positive law systematically, thus making it more intelligible to women. Within social security law this would, for example, contribute to less under-use of social security benefits among women. From social research we know that under-use of social security is a larger problem than misuse, even though misuse attracts greater attention, e.g. in discussions on unwed mothers' alleged abuse of social security. Systematizing birth law will in like manner lay the foundation for increased attainment of rights for women giving birth, and so on.

A systematic classification based on time-honoured principles offers both ease of understanding for those who learn rules of law and the possibility for those who apply them to find their way through the material. But the duty of legal science goes further. It also seeks to find new connections in law and society. This *theoretical* work does not operate primarily within existing frameworks, but rather seeks beyond them, crossing into other

spheres. The defining of new problem areas, radically changed
systematics, ideology critical analyses—all characterize this theoretical work. The concepts upon which each and every theory,
as well as legal theory, builds its statements become especially
prominent in this respect. We must therefore say more about
the role of concepts in legal theory generally and in women's
law specifically.

2.3. New Disciplines—New Concepts

Today 'conceptualism' has a negative connotation. Most are
of the opinion that both the so-called constructive school of
jurisprudence and the concept-oriented direction prior to it, lost
their way in logic and semantics, became slaves to their own
concepts when interpreting existing law, and therefore alienated
themselves from the reality they were meant to serve. There is
conceivably much truth in this criticism. There are times, however, when something fundamentally new is created, that one is
forced to systematize in new ways and to create new concepts.
In women's law such attempts resulted in a relatively large
growth of new concepts coinciding with the hypotheses and
results that the systematic feminist perspective provided. By
'concepts' we mean models that we through trial and error have
used along the road from hypothesis to theory.

This trial and error can either be based on impression and
conviction, or be based on empirical or dogmatic examination.
As knowledge and understanding increase, the process of trial
and error must continue to adapt accordingly. Changing contents thus does not necessarily mean that the concepts are not
good, but rather that they are developing through concept
formation with the aim of understanding connections between
rules, and between rules and reality. Often one goes from a
narrow definition to a broader one. At other times the concepts
will become more limited, being supplemented by others. In
women's law, for example, the concept 'equal status' is split
into de jure and de facto equal status (see chapter 3.4).

In the early stages concepts contain hypotheses about which
phenomena hang together and ought to be placed in the same
category. The women's law hypothesis about a 'law of birth' is
built upon a long row of fragmented rules which especially

concern pregnant and childbearing women. It is due to the fact that these fragments are gathered and seen in context that the concept 'birth law' originates (Fastvold 1977). The hypothesis is tested and the contents of the concept are changed and made more precise; gradually many more ideas are drawn under the concept 'birth law' (see chapter 5.3 for more detail).

When concepts are given a more precise content, they can develop from hypotheses to models which we through trial and error use to build theories. Theories show us rules of law, 'not isolated, but in their systematic context, not like a motley multitude of dissimilar arbitrary commands, but as applications or variations of certain simple fundamental principles' (Hagerup 1888:38). The theory in women's law of 'the tripartite support system for women', for example, ties together different sets of 'money law' rules: rules about the private duty of support in a marriage, about public assistance, and about payment for work (see chapter 6).

Women's law is built in part upon *new* concepts: birth law, equal status law, housewive's law, paid-work law. To some extent it utilizes *old concepts* which are infused with new contents, distilled and crystallized out from a new perspective. This applies for example to the concepts of 'equality' and 'discrimination', which are so fundamental to the logical reasoning in women's law that they deserve a special place for discussion and explanation (see chapter 3 for further details). The same applies to several of the concepts applied in the discussion of women-centred policy considerations, i.e., the basic values in women's law which bind together all of its tasks from definition of problems to systematics, evaluation and interpretation (see chapter 5).

By and large it is this concept formation which entitles us to talk about women's law as a new academic discipline—as opposed to a perspective within the study of law.

Many of the new academic disciplines which have become a part of post-World-War-II Norwegian law originated from the need to specialize, owing to the escalation of legal material and the growing number of legal relations within a social machinery perceived as progressively more complicated. Perhaps one could also say that the discipline of women's law originated because women in more and more areas of society have been leaving traditional roles and developing new ones. These new roles entail a rapidly rising number of new relationships in private life, work life and public administration. Women's law too can therefore function as a mere specialization if one is content with applying a feminist perspective within prevailing systematics thereby supplementing traditional fields by filling in intellectual vacuums and intellectual voids. But the aim of the discipline is obviously far more sweeping.

The unbroken cross-section through rules of law indicates in itself the discipline's holistic character. The totality is emphasized when knowledge from the discipline's juridically interdisciplinary work is combined and explained within the even more comprehensive structures of sex and society. Several sets of theories are necessary for this: theories of law and society (legal theories), women and society (feminist theories) and women and law (women's law theories). With respect to such tasks women's law will have several features similar to other holistic-oriented disciplines, for example, legal philosophy and general legal method.

3

Discrimination and Equality

Discrimination means differential treatment. Sex discrimination means differential treatment because of sex, for example rules and actions that treat men and women differently on the basis of their sex. Rules and actions that treat women and men differently on other grounds are not ab initio sex discrimination, since the intention has not been to treat them differently on the basis of sex. But such rules and actions can in fact have sex discrimination as a consequence. Since women's law is particularly concerned with law's consequence for women, we apply a broad meaning to the concept 'discrimination' so that it encompasses both direct and indirect discrimination, i.e. both law's (and action's) manifest and latent functions.

3.1. The Concept 'Sex Discrimination'

The concept 'discrimination' is itself neutral. There is nothing wrong with treating two properties or two phenomena differently, provided they are different and there exist good or acceptable reasons for the different treatment. In fact differential treatment in many situations is a necessary tool to create greater equality, but in normal usage the term 'discrimination' has a negative connotation, especially when the word is used in connection with sex, race or certain social traits of persons or groups. In normal usage one therefore often thinks of pejorative discrimination when the term 'sex discrimination' is used.

The concept 'sex' is also neutral in itself. But when we use the word in the context we have been referring to, it is most often the female sex that one has in mind, so that the concept 'sex discrimination' usually carries the meaning of invidious discrimination directed against individual women or women as a group.

A special problem arises when women are discriminated among themselves. Such discrimination is not *necessarily* sex discrimination, just as discrimination among men is not usually due to the fact that they are male. However, such discrimination among women often has its origin in the more ubiquitous sex discrimination generally found in society.

Some women live 'typical' women's lives, with continuous commuting between housework and paid work, combining the two in different proportions throughout various stages of life. Other women live lives more similar to those of men. This can have legal consequences for them, their children and other persons close to them, and most often those consequences are such that women who are most similar to men acquire the best legal rights and privileges.

The National Insurance Act's regulations for supplementary benefits for handicapped children illustrate this particular sex-linked discrimination among women—and even among their children.[1] The legal provisions which authorize the award and calculation of this supplementary benefit are technically gender-neutral. However, in practice they concern almost without fail the child's mother. This practice in effect entails an unreasonable and inappropriate discriminatory valuation of women's work of care and nursing based on a male model—whether the mothers have education, careers, other children, other duties of care, possibility for employment in the area they live in, etc. In earlier days the handicapped child's right to social security benefits at all was determined on the basis of whether the mother possessed or lacked the above-mentioned characteristics (see chapter 7).

The example shows the consequences that sex discrimination can have for society. Even though there is nothing stated in the National Insurance Act on this matter, and only hinted at in the

---

1. The National Insurance Act came into effect on 1 January 1967, and replaced the previous schemes relating to old age pensions, disability benefits, widows' and mothers' pensions, survivor benefits for children and rehabilitation assistance. Since 1 January 1971, health insurance, unemployment insurance, and occupational injury insurance have also been covered by the National Insurance Act.

legislative history, the full effect of this discrimination appears in the application of the law. Most often it is women in traditional sex roles who are effected by discrimination. At other times, however, problems can arise because most women live mixed and complicated lives—they live neither like 'typical' men nor like traditional women. Since the law in many instances is formed dichotomously—according to a 'man's model' and a 'woman's model'—there is a risk for many women that they can fall outside of the rules. Women become, more easily than men, the exception to the law (Sverdrup 1982).

3.2. Negative and Positive Discrimination

We distinguish between negative and positive discrimination when we evaluate the aim and consequence of the discrimination. It will always be the case that negative discrimination against one sex, directly or indirectly, means positive discrimination for the other, and vice-versa.

Let us use the Compulsory Military Service Act of 17 July 1953, No. 29, as an example. In section 3 it states that Norwegian male citizens are required to do military service; the corresponding provision concerning home guard service is the Home Guard Act of 16 July 1953, No. 28, sections 4 and 5. If one looks at the performance of military service as a duty, this rule contains negative discrimination against men, and simultaneously a positive discrimination in favour of women, who are exempted from such duty. However, if performance of military service and home guard service is viewed as a right—a right to protect the nation on equal terms—this rule would amount to positive discrimination in favour of men and negative discrimination against women, since women cannot themselves choose whether to perform such service.

Prohibiting women from working in high civil service positions, as the law did until 1902, was not only negative discrimination against women, but also positive discrimination in favour of men. High civil service positions were reserved for 'Norwegian citizens', which was interpreted as 'Norwegian men'. In other laws the positive discrimination is directly expressed, such as when Article 6 of the Constitution prescribes agnatic inheritance to the crown. This positive discrimination in favour of princes is also negative discrimination against the royal princesses.

The systematic feminist perspective of women's law focuses upon discriminatory rules, whether negative or positive, and their relationship to women. It is this aspect of the rules we treat by examining discrimination among different groups of women or between women and men. This means that we do not always express the effect, if any, that the discrimination simultaneously poses for men. It is implicit that negative discrimination against women is usually advantageous to men, while positive discrimination for women usually means giving women special advantages to the detriment of men. As a rule such affirmative action for women is only detrimental to the legal rights of certain individual men and does not involve negative discrimination against men as a group. The reason for this is that positive discrimination in favour of women often has its background in women's weaker start and subsequent position, which is precisely what one attempts to counter-balance through affirmative action.

A controversial example is the rule in section 11 of the Child Benefits Act (24 October 1946, No. 2), which states: 'If both parents are responsible for the care of the child, the child benefit is to be paid to the mother.' When the Government in the 1960s proposed to repeal the rule in favour of gender-neutral rules granting tax deductions for supporting children, there appeared an unexpectedly strong female opposition to the proposal. The child benefit proved to be the only independent source of money that many women had—even though it was supposed to be applied to the child.

The Government's proposal would have meant a strengthening of the family's economy in that generally the tax deduction for a supported child was to exceed the loss of the child benefit. It was not, therefore, the loss of money to the family that women protested against, but the loss of a gender-specific cash payment. Women were given the right to this cash payment after World War II, in recognition of women's closer ties to children, and in the belief that the money would most likely come into the right hands. It was thus not women's weak position after the war which gave impetus to the rule. However, it was an expressed weak position in the 1960s that gave impetus to maintaining the rule. Since then no one has dared to propose that the child benefit be abolished, even though it can be said to have been gradually undermined by the proliferation of tax deductions for supporting children, which have far outstripped the increase in child benefits (Dahl 1980 a).

Positive discrimination in favour of women often has its foundation in women's reproductive functions. In some cases this involves rules that naturally cannot apply to men—for example certain regulations in the Law on Abortion or the right to breast feed in section 33 of the Working Environment Act. In such cases it is not natural to speak of positive discrimination. Whether one uses the term 'women' or a gender-neutral term, such a set of rules would necessarily benefit only women. But there is a thin line between rules that are by nature gender-specific rules and those that are characterized by a combination of biologically gender-specific rules and rules founded upon cultural privileges and protective legislation. Several of these special protective regulations in the Working Environment Act and the National Insurance Act apply only to women. Others apply to both women and men, but give women greater rights, for example, the right to maternity/paternity benfits during maternity/paternity leave for infant care after birth, see the National Insurance Act section 3-21. But these greater rights are grounded in women's connection to and labour involved in childbirth, breast feeding and child care, thus grounded in women's strengths, rather than in their weaknesses.

Regulations governing public or private pension funds and the National Insurance Act's survivors' benefits have, on the other hand, previously favoured widows more than widowers, the reason being that widows were generally in a weaker economic position than widowers.

There are far fewer areas of life where positive discrimination in favour of men would have a neutral or reasonable effect on women as a group than vice-versa, since law generally has a content and a structure that favours men's lives, attitudes and conditions. This is also recognized in the Equal Status Act of 1978. In its preamble, section 1, it states that the law 'shall improve equality between the sexes and shall have as its specific goal the improvement of the position of women'. In accordance with this, section 3 makes possible both the maintenance and enactment of discriminatory regulations which, in accordance with the legislative intent, improve equality between the sexes. That means generally that there would be stronger arguments for positive discrimination in favour of women, and thus indirect negative discrimination against men, than vice-versa— since the law is specially directed to improving the position of women.

There was a certain amount of controversy surrounding these issues when the Equal Status Act was enacted in the 1970s. The approach emphasized in the original draft was to fight discrimination in a completely neutral fashion. The gender-specific intent—to improve the position of women in society—was evident only from the purely introductory remarks of the first *travaux préparatoires,* while the selected examples which followed to a large extent dealt with the dangers of negative discrimination against men and the unreasonableness of this. According to the draft, neither positive nor negative discrimination was to be permitted other than in some few situations, limited to those situations concerning factors such as unequal physical strength, reproduction and public modesty. The declaration of the legislative intent and the greater possibility to discriminate in accordance with the intent first appeared in the law after pressure from the women's movement (Dahl et al. 1975).

During the 1970s most western countries enacted general sex-discrimination legislation, first and foremost in the area of employment, and they all raised, for the most part, the same fundamental questions. Over time there has grown up a copious literature about this new form of sex-discrimination legislation, about the laws, and about the origin of the laws and their consequences.[2]

Quotas are a relatively new form of affirmative action for women. They appear in two very different varieties; allocation quotas and priority quotas. An example of an allocation quota would be the requirement that at least 40 percent of the repre-

---

2. The Norwegian debate is summarized in Halvorsen 1982, 1985; Holgersen 1984; Skjeie 1982; Dahl et al. 1975. The Swedish situation is treated in Widerberg 1980; Dahlberg 1980, 1983; Berge 1982; Westerhäll-Gisselsson 1979 chapter 2. For Danish law see: Nielsen and Thorbek 1976; Nielsen 1981; Edelberg 1981. Finnish law: Bruun 1982; Eriksson 1984.

sentatives of a political party or organization must be women. (The rule is often formulated neutrally, i.e. by stating that 'each sex' must be represented by at least such and such a percent, in this case 40 percent).

Allocation quotas can be used for the intake of a specific number of persons to specific positions, for example the admission of students to school, the choice of delegates to a national convention, or the listing of candidates on an election list.

A 'priority quota' is exemplified by the practice at some institutions of higher education that under certain conditions, the admission of female applicants is to take precedence over the admission of male applicants. The conditions can be 'moderate' or 'radical', i.e., it can be decided that female applicants with qualifications equal to male applicants shall have priority (moderate), or that female applicants shall have priority if they satisfy the minimum requirements for the position, even though male applicants may have better qualifications (radical) (Skjeie 1985).

The use of quotas has, however, been rather limited, and then usually as a self-imposed obligation upon the institution or organization in question. To what extent a decision to use quotas in fact bestows 'rights' is unsettled and is not so likely to arise, except in the rare case where an institution has imposed upon itself a 'radical' priority quota for filling a specific position. If a woman is first deemed competent in such a case, then she is entitled to the position, and can appeal against being passed over for a male applicant e.g. to the ministry in question. However, with the different varieties of 'moderate' priority quota, experience shows that the problem of two or more applicants having exactly 'equal qualifications' seems never to arise (Skjeie 1985, Halvorsen 1985).

The use of allocation quotas proves to be effective politically for women, provided that associations and parties follow the decisions of their central authorities. However, during the nominations for the parliamentary election in 1985, Sogn and Fjordane County branch of the Labour Party refused to submit to the party's central authorities' demand that at least 40 percent of the nominations on the election list be filled by female candidates, and the county could not be forced to nominate anew. Such conflicts are significant for the outcome of the election, because if all the parties had the same requirement and the local branches complied, almost half of the representatives in parliament would be women, yet according to law there is very little regulation or enforcement of a party's or association's internal rules, at least thus far. In quite a different position is the duty to have women comprise at least 30 percent of all appointments that the Government imposed upon itself in the form of two royal decrees in 1973 and 1976 respectively (Hernes 1982 a:81), the principle of which later became codified in section 21 of the Equal Status Act. Section 21 imposes a legal duty upon the Government to fill all public boards and councils with a certain percentage of women.

The use of quotas is extremely controversial. Its opponents fear that unqualified women will fill positions that they cannot master. Its proponents believe that qualifications are in general equally spread among the sexes, and that the use of quotas will thus raise the quality of those who get the position.

3.3. Sex Discrimination in the Law

De jure sex discrimination is sex discrimination in the law, i.e., laws that expressly treat men and women differently.

Some legal provisions of this type have been interpreted so as in fact not to treat men and women differently: the discriminatory passages are simply considered relics from the days when persons in public affairs and in the law were usually men. We had for example such a law until 1978. The third paragraph of section 5 of the Wine and Spirit Monopoly Corporation Act of 19 June 1931, No. 18, stated that: 'The King is to appoint a business*man* as administrative director'. The law certainly did not—at least not in its latter years—prohibit the appointment of a woman, even though such an appointment has not yet occurred. The opposite interpretation would—at least in post World War II Norway—be unreasonable, and might even be said to have been beyond the intent of the legislators at the time the law was enacted, making the use of gender-specific language here more a form than an act having legal consequences. The greater concern is that society has many such forms which in themselves create a pattern of behaviour and thus offer a social reality of limited expectations and thereby also few opportunities for women to obtain leading positions in society. However, the statutory forms have also sprung out of the harsher reality of a time when women did not have access to education and positions in public life.

It is less clear what happens in the case of a legal provision such as that on pimps which states that 'a man who wholly or in part is supported by a woman who engages in prostitution, is to be punished ...' (section 206, paragraph 3, of the Criminal Code). In view of the constitutional prohibition (Article 96) against conviction except according to law, it is highly questionable whether a woman who under similar circumstances is supported by a man, could be punished according to this law. It is just as doubtful whether a man who is similarly supported by a man, or a woman by a woman, could be punished. There are many possibilities here. In some of the constellations a court might explain away the gender issue—even though involving criminal punishment—by emphasizing the public policy argument that changes in society have broadened the applicability of the law. It is and would be nevertheless clear that it was the gender-specific pimp-prostitute relationship between man and woman that the legislators intended to eradicate when the law was enacted.

A third type of legislation which discriminates on the basis of sex is the law where nature itself grounds the gender-specific application of the law. In the Act on Termination of Pregnancy of 13 June 1975, No. 50 (the Abortion Act), women are central in two ways. Firstly in that it is, of course, only women who can abort. But also in that the woman is given the sole decision-making authority over the question of abortion up to the first 12 weeks of pregnancy, provided important medical reasons do not militate against this. In addition, the woman has a significant voice in the joint (doctor-patient) decision on the question of abortion after the first 12 weeks of pregnancy, see the Law on Abortion, section 2 (Olsnes 1985). Here, one can well imagine that women as potential mothers may not have had such a strong legal position. It was not until 1978 that the rules were changed from a right of consultation to a right of self-determination in the first phase of pregnancy, and even then under strong opposition from people who considered reproduction a societal or divine concern more than an individual choice. When the right to self-determined abortion was first proposed in the Labour Party's Report on the Family of 1974, it was not only the doctor who had a say in the decision. The potential father of the child was also to be consulted.

The Abortion Act also has provisions in which the different treatment of the sexes could very well have been given less weight. Section 14(a) states for example that a woman who has had an abortion *shall* pursuant to law be assured information about methods of birth control when she requests it, while the man's right to such information is weaker and is based on section 1. Section 1 states that society 'to the extent it is possible', shall insure children all the necessities of a good upbringing, and as a result 'shall insure that all persons receive ethical guidance on sexuality, information about questions of living together, and advice on family planning'. This provision must, however, be interpreted as a declaration of policy and thus does not give individual rights such as the right to information on birth control given to women in section 14(a).

Finally it must be pointed out that the text of statutes often has a masculine character because the word 'he' is used as a common reference to women and men. However, the Ministry of Justice is now trying to avoid this practice.

On the other hand, we have certain laws which have long used a gender-neutral form, but whose applicability through history have been gender-specific. Section 192 of the Criminal Code on rape is a good example: 'The person who with violence, or by instilling fear for *one's* life or well-being, forces *someone* to sexual intercourse, or is an accomplice to it, is to be punished ...' (my italics). The perpetrator, the victim, and the accomplice to the crime can all be viewed technically as either a man or a woman. But the provision is, according to its legislative intent, directed towards men who rape women.

More conspicuous, however, than the remaining laws and expressions which discriminate on the basis of sex are the parliamentary efforts in recent years to purge the law of such statutes and expressions. During the latter half of the 1970s, law after law was changed with the aim of obtaining statutory equality for women and men, without anyone attempting to assess more closely the policy considerations that might have been grounds for keeping such laws (see Widerberg 1980, chapter 6, for Swedish Law).

A new creation in Norwegian law is a particular type of sex-discrimination prohibition, modelled on that found in the Equal Status Act, which seems to be finding its way into various other unrelated statutes. These proscriptions are often formulated neutrally and directed against the 'disparaging characterization of a particular sex', while the legislative histories show that it is especially the disparagement of *women* that the statutes are concerned with.

Section 1 paragraph 2, of the Marketing Control Act of 16 June 1972, No. 47, states:

> Advertisers and those who design advertisements shall make certain that the advertisement does not conflict with the mutual dignity of the sexes, and that it does not give the impression of a disparaging characterization of a particular sex nor portray in an offensive manner either woman or man.

Both the expressions 'mutual dignity of the sexes' and 'disparaging characterization' involve a reference to norms which can be formulated as gender-neutral. The legislative histories express concern for preventing 'invidious' or 'degrading' sex-role characterizations or disparaging remarks such as statements like 'women are unpractical', or 'men are rude'. The Ministry of Consumer Affairs and Government Administration's report 'Advertisement and Sex' (NOU 1981:16), which orients advertisers and administrative enforcement officials to the implication of the new law, establishes quite clearly, however, that it is discrimination against women, and not general sex discrimination, one seeks to eliminate. This is clearly manifested in the prohibition against the offensive portrayal of men or women. Here the legislative history refers explicitly to the 'portrayal of women in a more or less undressed state, the woman depicted as a sexual object or as an eye-catcher' (ibid: 8).

Similarly, in the Criminal Law Advisory Council's report on 'Pornography and Punishment', submitted on 12 March 1985, a proposed new section 377(a) in the Criminal Code would forbid the exhibition of pictures of naked persons 'which gives the impression of a disparaging characterization of a particular sex or portrays in an offensive manner either woman or man'. From the Advisory Council's general comments it is evident that it is pornography's 'offensive and disparaging view of women', its 'contempt for women', which lies beneath the proposal. The Advisory Council's intention was to evaluate pornography on the basis of its presumed harmful effect, not as in the past, on the basis of moral standards. The nature of pornography is the oppression of woman. From this premise the Council concluded that 'pornography to many women [is considered] offensive—and to a certain degree even threatening. In this respect pornography has harmful effects on women' (Criminal Law Advisory Council 1985:77).

In the light of these examples one can claim that the neutral prohibition against offending the one or the other *sex* which is more and more often appearing in Norwegian law, applies in actuality to various situations of society's discrimination against *women*. Why legislators choose to fight women's oppression with gender-neutral language, as opposed to drawing their expressions from the circumstances which are in fact the bases for the decision to intervene, may be due to the traditional use of gender-neutral language in legislation which has long been visible in Nordic countries. Karin Widerberg's investigation of gender-neutralization in Swedish legislation from 1750 to today establishes that this tendency was noticeable from the middle of the nineteenth century. Although in the beginning it was done out of motives other than the interests of women and equality, and although interrupted by legislation designed to protect women employees by special treatment, Swedish law has tended to strive for gender-neutral language. But it was not until the 1970s that gender-neutralization—as in Norway—became a systematic policy, grounded in considerations of equality and implemented with the aim of improving the position of women (Widerberg 1980).

3.4. De Jure Equality, De Facto Discrimination

The term 'de facto discrimination' means that we aim at the *consequences* of both law and the application of law. Technical equality can have de facto discrimination as a result, just as discrimination can promote de facto equality.

Generally, the twin concepts 'law in books' and 'law in action' are essential to research in women's law. The situation today is that little discrimination remains in the statute books. Why absurd consequences nevertheless occur resulting in differentiation between the two sexes, despite de jure equality, is one of the most important themes in women's law.

The Equal Status Act too, which in its main clause prohibits discrimination against women and men, emphasizes its application to situations where the consequences are discriminatory and not only where the action itself is discriminatory. According to section 3, paragraph 2, 'the term "discrimination" means an action which treats men and women differently because of their sex. Discrimination also includes an action whose *effect* in fact works in such a way as to unreasonably render one sex worse off than the other' (my italics).

The statutory definition indicates two seemingly rather different types of discrimination. The first sentence concerns an action which treats men and women differently because of their sex, i.e., direct discrimination. The second sentence concerns indirect discrimination where the action in itself can hardly be characterized as discrimination, but where the effect of the action leads to the sexes being in fact situated differently, i.e. formal equality harbouring de facto discrimination.

The statutory definition therefore encompasses both direct discrimination and technically equal treatment, provided the action results in de facto discrimination. The primary criterion of whether there exists a violation of law is in both cases the action's discriminatory *effect*. But the degree of discrimination necessary to satisfy the statutory definition is different in each case. According to the first sentence, it is sufficient that the action 'treats women and men differently because of their sex'. According to the second sentence, a qualified negative consequence is required, i.e., that the one sex is unreasonably rendered worse off than the other.

As regards direct discrimination, the reasons or motives for the action are a central criterion, as well as the consequences of the action. It is only actions which treat women and men differently *because of their sex* which are prohibited, not unequal treatment based on other grounds. When a man is hired instead of a woman because he has better qualifications, this does not amount to discrimination within the meaning of the first sentence of section 3, paragraph 2, even if the guidelines establishing qualifications are formulated in such a way that it is generally men who satisfy the qualification requirement. If such an action is to be prohibited, it must fall under the second sentence of section 3, paragraph 2. This would in fact be the case if the guidelines for employee qualifications were formulated in such a way that equal treatment in accordance with them amounted to an unreasonable systematic exclusion of women. This is not a rare occurrence (Halvorsen 1985).

We see in this example how illusory the border can be between the negative consequences of unequal treatment and the negative consequences of technically equal treatment, even though the categories seem to be different. We see also that in practice it can be unnecessary or unreasonable to draw a distinction here, at least when drawn according to the principles of the Equal Status Act.

What is said here about discriminatory *actions* is equally applicable to discriminatory *rules*.

Section 16, paragraph 5, of the Taxation Act officially treats the division of income from a husband and wife's joint business without consideration of gender. The provision uses the gender-neutral term 'spouse'. However, in reality there is a question whether this provision systematically places women, and especially farm-women, in a worse position than men.

The gender-neutral term 'spouse' is from experience one of the most gender-specific words in the law. There is almost always an interesting women's law problem behind the application of the term 'spouse'. The consequence of section 16 of the Taxation Act is that it in effect discriminates against women.

The main rule of section 16 is that the income of a joint business 'is considered to be earned in its totality by *the spouse who* must be regarded as the *real executor* of the work' (my italics). One of the spouses is as a start pointed out as the 'real executor', and that will in almost all cases favour the husband over the wife, if only because the work of childbirth and child care interrupts her routine activity. Even though they work in a business which is a joint enterprise—for example a farm—it is the husband who from the start is awarded the benefits of being regarded as the earner of the total income, with all the consequences this has, such as the right to, and amount of, sickness benefits and other Social Security benefits. Having taxable income within the meaning of the Taxation Act is not only an economic benefit, for example, with respect to Social Security benefits.

The effect of section 16 is that it values women's and men's work differently, with the consequence that also has for the way each sex views itself and the other. This effect is reinforced by the further provisions in section 16, paragraph 5, which make possible the truncated valuation of women's work. The spouses can demand separate assessment for 'a suitable amount of the surplus', according to the amount of work each of them has contributed to the enterprise, unless the tax authorities find that such a limitation would be 'obviously unfair'. The tax authorities have so far been exceedingly strict in the practical use of this exception (Rognlien 1977). This means that the man's work on a middle-sized family farm or a large farm (with employed labour) is generally valued quite differently, i.e., higher than the woman's work, and this is so throughout one's entire life. He earns pension points for a higher old age pension, while she will seldom rise over the basic minimum pension.

3.5. Law and Life

Injustice occurs in practice, behind the facade of rights and privileges officially guaranteed to everyone. It occurs in the form of discrimination in enforcement, such as unfairness in the decisions of courts and other administrative authorities, or in the form of social and economic barriers to the fulfilment of rights and privileges. It can occur simply because the different sexes live such different lives that the substance of the rules on the whole rarely function justly for persons of a particular sex.

This relationship between 'law in books' and 'law in action' (terms used by American legal realists of the 1930s) has been formulated through history in many different ways. In the sociology of law—especially in Nordic countries—this applies in a broader sense to the entire complex of law and society. All directions of legal theory address this relationship, either as an essential and explicit theme, or as an underlying premise. The writer on legal doctrine emphasizes the application of law based on the text and legislative intent. The more consequence-oriented legal scholar wants laws across the board to be evaluated on the basis of their effect, not only in individual cases, but also their effects as a collective whole manifested throughout the entire process of legislation, interpretation and application. In the shadow of criminal law there has developed an entire academic discipline—criminology—which seeks to deal with such problems. Moreover, the entire spectrum of critical, materialistic and marxist legal theory has the relationship between law and society as a main theme of investigation.

It is the same complicated interplay between law and life that is being researched in women's law. We do this with the aim of achieving a more reasonable and just legal system, evaluated on the basis of the interests of women. These interests can be promoted with the use of arguments founded on equality, whether or not derived from the Equal Status Act. The visible instance of obvious discrimination should be judged on the basis of society's general norms of *equality* and *equality of treatment*. One can say that the differences between the sexes which these arguments address are precisely the differences that these arguments seek to minimize in order to be effective.

It is clear that this work draws a line where law and life apparently separate. For example, the legislative history of the Marketing Control Act states that the law's prohibition of advertisement 'in conflict with the mutual dignity of the sexes' (section 1, paragraph 2) applies to the kind of advertisement that contributes to the maintenance of invidious sex roles. However, advertisements which show women busily occupied with cleaning and washing, or advertisements where mother sews while father reads are considered difficult borderline cases because they can be said to portray reality as it is, or as many believe it to be. In the view of the Ministry of Consumer Affairs and Government Administration it is not considered worthy of criticism 'if an advertisement portrays women performing household chores. Such an advertisement says nothing about whether or not men participate in housework. Furthermore, a ban against such advertisement would be a disparagement of important social duties'. (NOU 1981:16, p. 8). The example is a good illustration of the limitations of equality arguments, and the regressive consequences that follow when one clings to such tenets, even though they lead to untenable positions.

According to an evaluation in women's law, discrimination against women penetrates far deeper than violations of an idealistic sex-discrimination statute. The relationship between law and society, law and life, are often far more complicated and full of contradictions than the promoters of sex-discrimination legislation suppose. The state of justice is influenced by a large number of factors, especially by economic and social factors which in reality decide the paths and conditions of women in society. Law has no clear role, either as an automatic reflection of society's norms or as useful social edification. Law can lag behind developments in both society and public opinion of what law is or ought to be, just as it can precede these. To improve the position of women with the help of the law necessarily means the development of a women's law with a foundation broader and different from sex-discrimination legislation and its possible derivatives in various special legislation. I will now give an overview of this foundation by examining the *sources* from which women's law flows, and the methods which the various sources demand for their analysis.

4

Sources and Methods

Problems in women's law come primarily from three fundamental sources, which demand different methodological approaches: (1) empirical data about the living facts of women in society and the operation of legal rules; (2) sources of law and legal doctrine; and (3) certain women-centred policy considerations.

Like other legal scholars, we raise problems which take as their starting point the positive law, and which apply ordinary methods of legal analysis. However, as indicated before, there are only a few marginal areas where legislation and judicial practice attribute legal significance to gender per se. The most interesting problems concerning the legal status of women therefore demand knowledge of women's lives and positions in society. Such knowledge must be gathered by empirical methods before we can examine how the living facts of society stand in relation to the law. The third source is our opinions of what the status of women is and ought to be, i.e., our ethical and political convictions, which both direct us, and present special problems, in the research of women's legal reality.

These three sources of problem-raising, each of which is connected to a principal methodology—the doctrinal, the empirical and the politico-theoretical—are also reflected in the stated objective of women's law outlined in chapter 1: to describe, explain and understand the legal position of women, with the specific aim of improving women's position.

Even though the primary sources and methodologies are different, there are unclear transitions and areas of overlap among them; they entangle each other in various ways. Women-centred policy considerations, for example, have their origin in moral philosophy and political ideology. Such policy considerations are found in systematic empirical information about women's moral and political convictions, or in more subjective sources. Such considerations do not just determine which problems are to be taken up, what criteria the law is to be judged by, and what kinds of reforms one might conceivably work for. They are also a part of fundamental sources of legal doctrine and may thus be significant for both interpretations and application of law. The women-centred policy considerations are in short the life blood and backbone of the various aspects of women's law, flowing to its outer reaches and uniting its interdisciplinary form.

4.1. The Empirical Starting Point

It is nothing new that a legal discipline should formulate a program linking it to empirical data or to policy considerations, in addition to maintaining its anchor in the more narrow legal doctrine. Francis Hagerup's one hundred years old 'synthetic method' involved an energetic extension of the basic methodology of legal doctrine, not only through its principal objective of constructing concepts and theories and binding rules together in a systematic whole, but also by giving the empirical element a central place in law (Hagerup 1888). The desire for a closer relationship to the empirical sciences had proved fruitful at the faculty of law in Oslo in the 1930s. Upon his retirement in 1933 Fredrik Stang proclaimed: 'never have there been more favorable conditions for a sociologically and economically focused legal science, and never before could it have had greater usefulness' (Stang 1933:130). Stang himself had led the way in creating a realistic commercial law. Later Ragnar Knoph worked to spread greater understanding of the significance of social considerations for themes in law, for legal form, and for the use of legal sources. Knoph was also the primary force behind the establishment of sociology of law as a discipline at the faculty of law.

In our time inspiration from both Norwegian and American realism of the 1930s has left its mark, first and foremost through Torstein Eckhoff's interest for the empirical study of law, especially the application of legal rules and their consequences. Together with Vilhelm Aubert, he developed consequence-oriented legal doctrine and sociology of law to such a level that he has influenced legal thought among many of today's legal scholars.

The connection between law and the other social science disciplines cannot, however, be said to be strong. There are several reasons for this. Firstly, the development of the various social sciences has not brought them closer to law. The tendency over time has, on the contrary, been that one discipline after another has grown away from the science of law and to some degree taken refuge in other faculties. Economics and political science have gone their own way. In the last few years even criminology has shown signs of distancing itself from its criminal law origin. The development of sociology of law has been more complicated. Within this field sociological methods and perspectives dominated for a while; however, one is now witnessing the emergence of a new generation of 'sociologico-jurists'; especially prominent are the works of Ståle Eskeland and Jon T. Johnsen.

The tendency towards separation of law and social science has led to counter-measures on the part of lawyers. During the development of the law of negotiable instruments and banking as a new discipline at the Faculty of Law in Oslo, Carsten Smith pointed out the necessity of connecting this discipline thematically and methodically to economics, so as not to 'risk that the law, and thus the principal legal reasoning in this field, like a burnt out rocket, follows a downward course' (Smith 1980:61). Erik Boe is one of the few who has made a conscious attempt at a methodological amalgamation of legal doctrine and social science in a large research project (Boe 1979). He has continued and expanded this program of integration in his new work on regional development under changing economic and political conditions (Boe 1985). Others have taken up similar themes to only a limited degree.

Eckhoff himself raises the question whether lawyers' present indifference to social sciences is connected to the social and human view of life prominent among lawyers, with their heavily rule-oriented view of reality: what you have rules about, is also found in reality. These weaknesses in the law

can only be remedied by gathering greater information about the existing qualities of life that are objects of regulation, and greater insight into the effects of the legal rules. In addition to this we need greater understanding of what it is that motivates human actions, and a holistic view of society which is not too strongly influenced by juristic prejudicates. To obtain this it is ... important to begin a rapprochement with other social sciences. (Eckhoff 1984:11).

When women's law originated as an academic discipline in 1975, it was associated from the start with the social sciences through its connection with women studies. This research had a heavily interdisciplinary orientation, and its data were perceived as a common good for all women researchers and lawyers.

For lawyers, however, there are special difficulties in the integration of these data, since legal method has requirements completely different to those of social scientific methods. In addition to the reciprocal use of social science data and women studies data in defining problems and constructing theories, women's law must seek its own data, based on the discipline's own methodological needs. This entails methodological aims and requirements different from sociology's usual representative sampling and validity requirements, or anthropology's and psychology's requirement of more precise qualitative data-gathering techniques.

Through the initiative of Free Legal Advice for Women (later JURK), the gathering of data on women's reality was combined with the offer of legal assistance, which proved to be well-suited to dealing with women's legal problems. The answers received through contacts with women throughout the country were, however, not representative, either geographically, socially, or with respect to age or subject-matter. And unrepresentative distribution in the offer of legal assistance led, of course, to unrepresentative distribution in raw data. This meant that we could utilize the information only so as to obtain an understanding of the *nature* and *variety* of women's legal problems. But this showed itself to be significant enough—and for a lawyer perhaps even more important than data on the representative characteristics of a problem area. Our method aimed to register the widest possible spectrum of legal problems, and afterwards to attempt to propose hypotheses about the more general connections, and eventually to test these against social science data and theories.

In addition, information had to be gathered in specific limited areas. The legal situation of employees in private homes was examined in this way, in order to analyze the rights and obligations of women who perform housework, care and nursing for others—outside the nuclear family, but within the home—for example domestic help, unskilled nurses, baby-sitters, and women cleaners. There were no sociological studies or statistics bearing directly on the subject. A number of baby-sitters, unskilled nurses and their employers were therefore sought out and interviewed. The interview form itself most closely resembled what sociologists call the qualitative method. The object was not to examine either quantitative or qualitative factors, but to obtain information relevant to the legal dialogue. The interviews offered ideas as to what aspects of the relationship the parties found problematic. Finally, it was possible to create a picture of the more social aspects of work conditions.

In comparison to what one might require of a sociological study, such as the ones conducted on the same topic in the comprehensive studies of Norwegian domestic help (Aubert et al. 1952 and the Committee for a Law on Domestic Help 1960), the empirical data were modest. But the method used resulted in the definition of new problems of great practical interest for women with respect to the questions of principle which arise concerning the legal regulation of care and personal relations. Tone Sverdrup describes how in this area we often find a 'lawmaker's dilemma' between government regulation and interpersonal relations. Exact rules conflict with the individual accommodation which is so important in such a relationship. Legal standards will, on the other hand, have no effect with respect to exploitation in an individual work relationship. Such legal rules are too imprecise, and often too devoid of substance, to be used directly by the parties. Legal standards need interpretation and are therefore best suited to more 'professional' enforcement (Sverdrup 1984a:108–9). To protect the weak party in the relationship, one must therefore seek legal safeguards which accommodate the interpersonal relationship, for example, the use of legislation that delegates broad regulatory powers, combined with specific and direct guidance to the parties as to what can reasonably be demanded of the other party. Such guidance can be supplemented by the offer of standard contract forms or the demand for the parties to enter into written contracts (ibid: 124 f).

The combination of data collection and the offer of legal assistance has proved to be especially fruitful. It contributes to the creation of a special relationship of trust, a dialogue in interview form which focuses the interviewee's attention on the legal aspects of her existence, something that enhances the interviewee's ability to respond in a more useful and relevant direction. In the housewife project on marital practices one sees how this method has provided the foundation for: (1) definition of problems, (2) interpretation, and (3) a use of legal sources (Hellum and Fastvold, 1985).

Women's law thus applies empirical social science research in several different respects: in part women studies help to define problems and set priorities for their treatment; in part the data and theories of various women studies' projects are applied in the interpretation and use of legal sources; and finally we ourselves gather data out of a juridically motivated need for empirical data. Empirical knowledge, consequently, plays a part in the definition of problems, concept and theory formation, interpretation of law, and also in legal politics. Women's law—in any case as it is practised in Norway—can thus be said to have empirically researched reality as its point of departure for legal analysis. Although legal doctrine certainly is most important, we seek to build upon empirical data in the description and evaluation of law. This is not meant to detract from the importance of being able to reason doctrinally in any given situation, but rather to replace a part of the ivory tower conjectures of traditional legal doctrine about actual facts with the revelations of empirical research.

4.2. Sources of Law

Legal doctrine is, as described in section 2.2, primarily the interpretation and application of existing law. It takes the positive law as its object, and its task is to examine and evaluate the general norms of written and unwritten law when faced with specific legal questions. Both the most central and the most peripheral of such concrete living facts shall be identified: the most central in order to draw out that which has practical value, the most peripheral in order to establish the borders of valid law.

The theory of sources of law prescribes a methodology for this interpretation process. It gives guidance as to which sources of law should apply, as well as rules governing their individual application and mutual harmonization. The universe of legal sources has naturally enough changed over time, specifically the type of sources and their mutual ranking order, but also with respect to which institutions making and applying the law are most important for the individual's procedural and substantive rights and liberties.

The legal sources of women's law have two special characteristics: the use of legal sources 'from below', i.e. custom and public opinion of what the law is or ought to be are accorded great weight, for example, in researching issues of family law and law of the private sphere in general; secondly, a heavy emphasis upon government administration. Administrative agencies play a large and growing role for all citizens. But there is reason to believe that administrative practice plays an especially large role for women—in any case, both the women's movement and women studies have focused special attention upon the formulation of guidelines and decision-making at that level. Social security research has, for example, been of principal importance to both women's sociological and legal research.

With its emphasis upon custom and public opinion of what the law ought to be as living sources of law, women's law in part harks back to an older source of law theory, which attributes greater weight to the individual's everyday life and practice than is usual today. I therefore find it appropriate to sketch the development of sources of law theory in general and show the place of women's law in it. Afterwards I will treat the fundamental sources of law, i.e., legislation, judicial decisions, and administrative practice separately (sections 4.3-4.5) and the remaining sources of law collectively (section 4.6).

In earlier sources of law theory (for example Aubert 1877, Hagerup 1888 and 1931, Platou 1915, Gjelsvik 1912 and 1968) one operated with two exhaustive sources of law: law and customs. The contents of both categories was extremely broad, which was made possible by extensive use of 'legal analogy' (Augdahl 1973). Many things were clasified as 'law' as a result of the theories and methods of interpretation, whereby extremely different factors were accorded weight. But to an even greater extent than law, 'customs' constituted an extremely broad concept, since it was the catch-all for all the legal creations that could not be traced to legislation. When one spoke of customary law, one had primarily in mind law created from the customs of ordinary people. The special interest in these originated from the traditions of the Historical School of Law, which viewed law as something that grew slowly out of the lives of the people, in much the same way as language does. According to this theory, the customs themselves were considered to be the fundamental source of the law. The doctrinal writer's task was thus to draw the line between customs that had become law (i.e., customs that were recognized as valid law) and other customs and practices of society. For a custom to enjoy the status of law it had to be (1) uniformly practised, (2) practised over a long period of time, and (3) practised under the belief that one was legally bound by it. In other words it was not simply required that a specific practice had developed, but also that the custom embodied the general belief among the people that the custom had become compulsory and had acquired the force of law. Public opinion of what the law was and opinions of mere influential interest groups were thus built into this requirement.

It is clear that a determination of what was customary law necessarily involved a large degree of discretion, belief and conjecture, since it was quite impossible for the most part to ascertain not only how people in fact behaved in an area, or how uniform and extensive the practice was, but also to what extent people felt compelled to behave as they did. With the use of such all-encompassing and unrefined categories to describe existing law, legal theory easily fell a victim to fictions and contradictions. On the one hand, one gave the impression that the solution to the controversy was always to be found in the law—that those applying the law and writers on legal doctrine objectively 'found' the law [the completeness of law theory]— while on the other hand the law was being created by 'the will of the people' or by different interest groups. According to such theory 'judicial decisions' became a factual expression—a kind of proof—that the custom had obtained the status of customary law (otherwise the decision would not have been as it was, unless it was wrong). But others viewed even the practice of courts or administrative agencies as parts of the public's customs themselves and thus as factors in the development of customary law. In other words one incorporated various types of practice within the concept 'custom', thus reckoning the practice of the courts (judicial decisions) and administrative authorities as parts of the general public's customs.

The earlier theory of 'Natur der Sache', 'the nature of the thing', was also incorporated into the concept 'custom', often with great latitude for application of legal analogies. Platou pointed out how 'the nature of the thing' was an expression often used, but unfortunately without clear notions of what was meant, and sometimes for lack of other arguments. More specifically, he showed how in every society there are always to be found certain historically produced norms (e.g. for the orderly transference and ownership of property, for situations of inheritance, for marriage, trade etc.), whose legal aspects would be determined by the nature of the relationships in question. 'Thus the existing circumstances themselves produce the legal rule that manifests itself in the daily practice of people, because the legal rule is a product of existing interests that it shall protect .... It is this "nature of the thing" that is the foundation of customary law' (Platou 1915:57–59). In today's terminology such practical, ethical and political considerations are embodied in 'policy's' factual and normative place both in legal doctrine and in the sources of law theory.

The earlier theory is thus illustrative of how the sources of law are comprised of extremely different 'data', from an empirical perspective: the text of the law, the legislative history, the conduct of citizens, the decisions and practices of the courts, the decisions and practices of different administrative agencies, the decisions and practices of politicians, and finally the evaluations which are the bases of the decisions and practices, i.e., evaluations of a moral, political and practical nature, both with respect to the contents of the law and with respect to society and to human coexistence.

Out of the strong legal realistic currents of more recent times, there emerged an urgent need to extricate and refine the two-compartment source of law theory. Per Augdahl started this (Augdahl 1961). Magnus Aarbakke (Aarbakke 1965 and 1966) and Johs. Andenæs were among those who followed up (Andenæs and Kvamme 1969), and Torstein Eckhoff brought to fruition the modern theory of sources of law that is applied today (Eckhoff 1971), and that is taken as a start when 'the new source of law theory' is discussed. This theory seeks to introduce the most systematic distinction possible between the many elements that in fact form the basis of legal decisions. The task of this general methodology to a great extent consists of description, discussion and evaluation of the sources individually. On the other hand, Eckhoff continuously emphasizes that in practice there are not and cannot be clear distinctions between the different elements. They merge continually with one another in various combinations. If law is to be useful, decisions must be made, and one seldom has the insight that the sources of law ideally require, such as knowledge of the society and of the beliefs and opinions of the people. Nor will a legal scientist have the time, energy or possibility to control and verify the opinions and assessments he uses as a basis for his doctrinal exercise. The aim must therefore be reduced to showing care and to finding a balanced and reasonable procedure for solving legal questions.

It is not simply the internal theoretical development that has led to new views of the sources of law desired and in fact applied. Society's development too has demanded change. Today when both the legislative branch and the executive branch produce legal sources in an abundance never experienced before, the significance of customs, manifested in the conduct and opinion of ordinary people, has been sharply reduced. Legislation is not the most important source of law simply because of its place in the legal hierarchy. Legislation today is also the fundamental source in the shaping of our type of state. Legislation is both the foundation and instrument of 'the rule of law' and the welfare state. As regards the relationship between the administration of justice and government administration in general, the latter is increasing in size and significance both beyond and at the cost of the former. While judicial decisions continue definitely to occupy a more important place in the legal hierarchy and methodology, general administrative agencies' application of law and regulation-making powers today are of greater significance for the procedural and substantive rights and liberties of the individual. While the legal system has become more and more comprehensive and complicated, the decisions of courts have declined in importance both quantitatively in that there are now fewer cases decided than before, and qualitatively in that the few controversies that are litigated to the highest court have a weaker effect than when the legal system was more uniform and escaped such frequent and abrupt changes as it suffers today. In many areas the significance of the administration's regulatory scheme has also increased as compared to the significance of legislation. In more modern legal science the interest in both administrative law in general and the administrative law of specialized fields has steadily increased, manifested by the rise and development of new legal disciplines, such as Social Security Law, Tax Law, etc. One also sees how both representatives of these disciplines and others are in the process of gradually changing the sources of law theory again by pointing out the significance of both lower court decisions and especially lower levels of administrative decision-making. Anna Christensen's empirical-dogmatic work on Swedish unemployment compensation with its introductory discussion of methods is a good example of this legal development (Christensen 1980).

Little remains of the traditional notion of custom. It continues to have importance within contract law in the form of usage, and within other areas of the market which have not been the object of government regulation. One can also conceive of the more traditional notion of custom within private life and one's immediate community of neighbours, i.e., sectors without much government regulation. One type of custom that has received special treatment, also in more modern sources of law theory, is local custom as the basis of rights of use. It is often a question of customs which have been traditionally important for people's everyday life, for example, the rights of cutting timber and fishing, duty to repair fences etc.—with a smooth transition to a more individualized basis for rights, such as certain types of public rights of common, immemorial usage, adverse posession, and contracts. But in all of these connections what is perhaps most interesting is the legal relevance of knowl-

edge about existing circumstances of life, rather than the discussion of customary law in the traditional sense.

In both developments within the sources of law theory—(1)
the increased legal and practical significance of lower instances
of decision-making and rule-making, and (2) the interest in
practice in areas of private life not yet touched by government
regulation—women's law is actively participating in bringing
about these changes. I will come back to that later.

4.3. Statutory Law and Administrative Regulation

A doctrinal writer will in most cases take his starting point in
the written law, for example taking a factual situation and
applying the law to the facts with the aim of finding a solution
to the legal question. Within legal reasoning it is this application
of abstract norms to the facts of an individual case which is
most important, and must be most important if the doctrinal
writer has a judge as his addressee.

Women's law has only to a small extent carried out judge-
oriented research. It has, to a much larger degree than is usual
in law, addressed itself to other practical consumers of legal
theory—politicians and women interest groups, administrative
agencies and legislators—with the aim of providing information
and evaluating existing law from a feminist perspective. In
addition, women's law has concerned itself with proposals for
reform and strategy for long-term change. The discipline has
therefore directed its attention more toward general features of
the abstract norm than toward individual legal controversies.
Considerable weight has been given to the contents and consequences of the law with respect to women as a group, rather
than to individual legal issues to which women are parties. This
focus upon the general rather than the specific, and upon the
group rather than the individual, is also determinative of the
methods we apply in the examination of legislation itself.

The individual case can, however, be a starting point. In an
analysis of the Taxation Act's concept of 'income' vis-à-vis the
law's rules on who is to be considered a 'family supporter' and
what is to be considered 'work', an individual case was taken
as a start. Through analysis of the legal issues raised in this
concrete fact situation, one could generalize from the conse-

quences of the individual decision so as to address a group problem, namely the question of unrecognized work performed in the home (care of children, the sick and elderly, as well as housework) and its lack of or meagre regulation, with the consequences that has for various groups of workers performing such tasks (Sverdrup 1985).

One could also start with the examination of the extremely varied practices of a chosen group of women concerning arrangements in their marriages as to the management of money necessary to run the household. Subsequently one could use the knowledge gained to interpret and better understand 'the duty of support' in section 1 of the Spouses Property Act. Such an approach would be directed to influencing legislative work in progress, and for its general information value for women, rather than for the purpose of mapping out a forensic application of the law (Hellum 1985).

The general relations on the group level are found more in the legislative history of laws than in the legislative intent or in the knowledge garnered from concrete individual applications of the law. The reasoning gleaned from the legislative history can be essential for an understanding of the meaning of the law and its intended impact upon society. This can include parliamentary debates and the political constellation behind them—used to supplement the doctrinal writer's interest in the general and specific legislative intent as well as in the reasoning and suggestions of the committee of experts. From this it is a natural transition to other sources, outside legislative history proper, which can contribute to putting the law or parts of it in its proper context. Such sources might include history and political science, and would entail going beyond the usual principles for the use of *legal* sources. We do indeed advocate the use of *other* sources. Comprehensive works on the *history* of legislation concerning such items as prostitution from the end of the nineteenth century to the present day, or marriage, or abortion, have been completed by women's law researchers with academic backgrounds other than in law. The authors, however, emphasize positive law more than is usual in historical and political science research (Melby 1980 and Gulli 1980).

In addition to (1) statutory law, (2) the legislative history, and (3) the political and ideological context surrounding the legislative history, administrative regulations are an important source of law. Administrative regulations can have an unimaginative, bureaucratic function, but also a more political design. In some cases administrative regulations adopted pursuant to law can have far more relevance for the understanding of a complex of problems than the text of the law itself.

4.4. Judicial Decisions

Women's law has until now been engaged only to a small extent with judicial decisions as a source of law, especially as regards the Norwegian Supreme Court and its creation of precedent. Only to a very small extent do women reach the Supreme Court. If one examines the volumes of *Norsk Retstidende* [the reports of the Norwegian Supreme Court decisions], one would immediately notice the disproportionate distribution of men and women as parties to controversies.

The figures are symptomatic of the more general complex of women and society, and women and law. Traditionally women's lives and problems belonged to the domestic/private sphere, while men 'owned' the public sector. But the contours and substance of the women's sphere, the family, has been shaped in the men's world—by the state, interest groups and the marketplace. History proves that the private and public spheres have not developed equally for women and men respectively. Man has in many ways functioned both as the family representative in the public sphere, and as the state's representative in the family, i.e., as family supporter, figure of authority, and judge. Thus, neither dualism nor complementarity are suitable concepts to describe the relationship and dynamics between the familial and public sphere. Rather, the relationship is hierarchical (Hernes 1982 a:13 f). This has traditionally made women participate in formal mechanisms for solving legal controversies to a much lesser degree than men, and in areas not concentrated on by men.

There is actually only one area of law where women and men quantitatively have equal positions as parties to legal controversies, and that is in questions connected to paternity and divorce (custody, child support, alimony and division of property). The practices in some of these areas have also been analyzed, for example custody suits (L. Smith 1980) and property rights in the family home (Thue 1983) etc., but without these works touching upon theories and views of women's law. The last few years have, however, witnessed an increased interest in the feminist and housewife perspective in family law and torts. Kirsti Strøm Bull and Asbjørn Kjønstad have, for example, in several works analyzed and evaluated case law concerning the legal effects of work in the home within marriage and non-marital cohabitation (Bull 1979, 1982, 1983 and 1985, Kjønstad 1984 a and b).

However, in one area women reach the Supreme Court to a far greater extent than men, namely as victims of sex crimes and to some extent crimes of violence. In these cases women are, however, witnesses and not a party to the trial. Consequently, they have for the most part had no right to influence the conduct of the trial, even though they may have contributed to the initiation of the prosecution, for example, by reporting a rape or a violent husband. Investigations have revealed the difficulties that women who report these types of crimes can have, in addition to the problems created by the attack itself (Vestergaard 1974, Lykkjen 1976, Rasmussen et al. 1982). This is the principal reason that so few violations of law are reported and prosecuted in these areas of criminal law, not only in Norway, but in many other countries. Both in Norway and in other countries data are gradually being found, revealing the widespread occurrence of these crimes, previously thought to be less common. Within the past 10 years the situation has changed somewhat as a result of frequent exposure of these criminal violations, with regard to both wife-beating and to some extent rape. Moreover, changes in the law have given the victim in rape cases a special position in the criminal law process, i.e., the right to legal assistance throughout the entire legal process paid for by the State, see the 1981 Amendment to the Criminal Procedure Act, sections 113 et. seq. Such rules contribute to making women's legal problems more visible, also at the Supreme Court level.

In general women's increase participation in the public sphere will gradually leave its mark, even on the distribution of women and men as parties to legal controversies—and as other participants—in the courts' administration of justice. Thus, it is conceivable that judicial decisions will have a greater relevance for women's law. Some have, however, raised the question whether the courts' conflict-solving principles do not to a great extent 'belong' to man, his history, culture and position of power. Ulla Jacobsen alleges this in her women's law perspective of civil and criminal procedure (Jacobsen 1982).

4.5. The Practice of Administrative Agencies

Women are more visible in the scheme of administrative practice than in the decisions of the judiciary. A large part of the decision-making of civil servants is in areas of social and economic rights and obligations between the individual and government, and in a welfare state women are, to start with, on an equal footing with men. Women's law problems often crop up in regard to the politics of both health and social welfare. Health matters are often related to women's special role in bearing and raising children, but also to the allocation of health services during sickness. Social welfare matters are connected to more general questions about women as clients in society, their client status expressing women's weak position in society. For example, social security benefits play a relatively larger role for women than for men, even though women's position in social security law is weaker than men's (Wærness 1982, Sverdrup 1984 b). In the area of health and social welfare women have many situations and problems that are made the object of regulation, and this is so to a different extent and in a different way than with men. Here lies also some of the explanation as to: (1) why women's law has until now been engaged more in the research of administrative practice, rather than judicial decisions, as a source of law, and (2) why questions of health law and social welfare law have had an especially prominent place in women's law research.

In addition to the Equal Status Ombudsman,[1] where the complaints of women are clearly the most dominant issues (Halvorsen 1985), the Social Security Tribunal is the administrative agency whose practice has been most relevant for

---

1. The Equal Status Ombudsman together with the Equal Status Appeals Board collaborate in the implementation of the Equal Status Act.

women's law, in regard to women's law's use of both the tribunal's internal precedent archive and its important decisions selectively published in *Sosial Trygd* (see for example Gjelsvik and Wankel 1980).[2] Moreover, several systematic investigations of the Social Security Tribunal's decisions have been undertaken in specified areas over specified periods of time, comprising whole series of the collected decisions of the Tribunal. This research has been directed more to identifying patterns of decision-making than to conducting a case-by-case analysis of their precedential effect or to giving advice to administrative agencies and courts as to how individual cases ought to be solved in the future (chapters 7 and 8).

Departmental circulars, administrative documents disseminating guidelines and directives, are a little recognized source of law in legal doctrine. One may question whether a discussion of their significance belongs to a discussion of law and administrative regulations or to a discussion of the practice of administrative agencies. Since the form of departmental circulars can be rather closely related to lesser detailed administrative regulations, there is reason to examine these legal sources together. Departmental circulars are not considered a legal source of great value, and there are good reasons for this if one has judicial decision-making in mind. But for an understanding of the law, the way it functions at lower levels of administration and thus in the real world, departmental circulars are important sources for the interpretation of law in practice and for the evaluation of the same. As for women's law, departmental circulars have proved to be most revealing—the gender-specific character of the law is far more conspicuous in such circulars than in the text of laws and their legislative histories.

Women's right to disability pensions according to section

2. In connection with the implementation of the National Insurance Act, the Social Security Tribunal was established to decide conflicts between the insured and the social security administration. The Tribunal is an independent administrative organ, but it has many characteristics of a court. It is thus not a part of the ordinary administrative hierarchy. The judges of the Tribunal are jurists, doctors, rehabilitation specialists and laymen. A decision of the Tribunal can be appealed to the ordinary courts, but of the more than 20,000 cases that the Tribunal has handled up to now, only 20 or so cases have been appealed to the ordinary courts and only one has reached the Supreme Court. In practice therefore the Social Security Tribunal is the highest instance for social security cases.

8-3 of the National Insurance Act can serve as an example. In the text of the law neither the words 'women' nor 'housewives' is mentioned; nor is the question of women's or housewives' right to disability pensions given any special attention in the legislative history, at any rate no particular guidance is offered as to present practice concerning the award of disability pensions to housewives. But if we look through the National Insurance Administration's archive of departmental circulars we find a thick manuscript with the title: 'Housewives and Disability'.[3] Similarly, the many departmental circulars through the years about the right of unwed mothers to different types of social security benefits have been indispensable for an understanding of the general rules and practical applications which have lain hidden behind the statutory rules in chapter 12 of the National Insurance Act.

Even public information pamphlets can have a similar significance, for example, the pamphlets written in connection with the 1978 amendment to the Abortion Act and published by the National Health Service (Olsnes 1985).

In all of these situations one seeks outside the usual sources of law (i.e., the text of statutes, administrative regulations, and the more recognized legislative history materials) in order to explain and understand the law, and even the evaluation of law in these situations to some extent employs empirical methods.

Since the practice of administrative agencies concerns so many women in so many different situations, there is a special need for a more doctrinal examination of and discussion of administrative practice. Such investigations can function both in advisory capacities and as control mechanisms over administrative agencies, at the same time as they can be enlightening for the public if communicated in a useful manner. However, such aims create particular source of law problems, which lead the legal scholar away from the case-oriented doctrinal analysis—to what extent depends upon what area of administration she is concentrating upon and what kind of questions she is taking up.

---

3. Social Security is administered centrally by the National Insurance Administration, which is the highest instance for administrative appeal in the ordinary administrative hierarchy. Its decisions may be appealed to the Social Security Tribunal.

On the one hand, the individual decisions and guidelines of administrative agencies must be accorded considerable weight, since they often concern areas of law where judicial control is not a realistic possibility. This is so because it is often not legally or practically possible, and even if it were possible, the group of judicially reviewed decisions sometimes have little practical significance (E. Smith 1979: 62 f). Administrative decisions within social security law offer a good illustration of this problem, and so does the practice of the equal status administrative authorities. If the Equal Status Act were given a traditional doctrinal analysis, many essential and practical questions would be by-passed, and such an analysis would be difficult to apply both theoretically and practically (see for example Holgersen 1984). I presuppose that the work of the Equal Status Ombudsman *has* a special source of law value, even though the Commission is formally and hierarchically weak. This is an area where the courts up to now have not come into the picture, nor can they be presumed to play any role in the future other than by way of exception. At present the Equal Status Appeals Board has not had very many cases, but those that exist have, of course, a special source of law value. However, the Commissioner's decisions are of interest when the outermost limits of the law are construed. The general provisionof the Equal Status Act, section 3, is a legal standard which is to be applied to some extent by reference to the other provisions of the Act, which also entail broad discretion. The Commission has gradually developed a staff of specialists in the field, whose practices and policies must be accepted to be well-reasoned and well-supported.

On the other hand, there are special reasons in such areas why precisely legal scholars should fill both an advisory and a watch-dog function with respect to principles of equality, justice, and other individual rights and liberties. This means that legal scholars should have a certain independence when it comes to drawing the limits of the law's application, even when one faces a very specialized administrative agency. This also means that the persons addressed in this type of legal analysis ought not to be judges, or at least that the question of the person to be addressed ought to be recognized in discussions and analyses of administrative law.

Subordinate administrative agencies should be subjected to a critical eye. When administrative practice is formulated by professionals who primarily do not have legal aspects and the effects of rule formation in mind, one must expect legal errors and positions that are legally questionable. Moreover, broad, administrative discretion entails considerable power and authority that ought to be kept within the frame of existing law (Boe 1979:155 f). Anna Christensen's study of Swedish unemployment compensation practices is an illustration of the need for checks on the execution of administrative authority (Christensen 1980). Large areas of social science research confirm this need, and it is essential to focus more on the concept of 'control' (E. Smith 1979:67) and the law's role as the protector of individual rights and liberties (Dahl 1983:13 f).

Administrative agencies can also exhibit too much caution in relationship to their fundamental legal authority. Marit Halvorsen's study of the practices of the Equal Status Ombudsman with respect to sections 4 and 5 of the Equal Status Act indicates this (see Halvorsen 1985).

One should search for a sources of law theory that is in general more suited to administrative agencies and their clients. Bent Christensen has advocated such a program in his book on 'The question of legal authority in administrative law', when he addresses himself to the first instance of administrative decision-making and applies sources to this end (B. Christensen 1980).

4.6. Customs, Public Opinion and Policy

Women's law has striven to find suitable methods for lawyers to identify customs and people's opinion of what the law is or ought to be. The concept 'domestic practice' is a category for a type of empirically based source of law whose aim is to add a factual dimension to the established sources of law. But they are primarily considered supplementary empirical factors—especially for use in the formation of legal rules, but also in the application of law—and not as a source of law that must fulfil specific requirements in order to be applied, in the way that earlier legal theory required of the concept of 'custom'.

We are once more concerned with questions where the three basic methods merge with one another. (1) Customs can to some extent be an independent source of law (but without the strict requirement imposed on them by earlier legal theory). (2) To some extent customs can be used as empirical factors in relation to other legal sources (for example as evidence of what people believe the law is or ought to be, or in an evaluation of the nature and development of policy). Customs can also be used as an instrument in more legal-sociological analyses containing an 'outside perspective' of law. (3) Customs can be used as an instrument for describing reality as a step in the process of general theory construction. The application would determine what kind of requirements were necessary for research. In other words we are talking about the legal importance of knowing the existing concrete qualities of life as a part of both doctrinal evaluations and analyses in the broader sense of the word. Different applications have different objectives, which dictate different relevance. But the lines between the various kinds of applications are unclear, and the different methods of application will often overlap one another. In what follows it is primarily the application of customs in theory construction and in broader aims of the science of law which are taken up, and not custom as an independent source of law.

Privacy and family life are areas that continue to have much in common with past social life and law. They are areas of judicial voids, or judicial weaknesses—without regulation, or in any event outside the application of the law (cf. the doctrine of right of privacy). The parties sort out their own affairs through custom and agreement. Recently some parts of daily life have indeed become more public—women, for example, report to the police and other authorities infringement upon their physical integrity, or demand that the principle of the Equal Status Act shall also be firmly introduced into private and family life.

Marital practices can be an important source for describing, explaining and understanding the law (among other things, by illuminating 'law in action' in relation to 'law in books') and the reasons why women's problems are regulated to a lesser extent than men's (Hellum and Fastvold 1985).

An example of this is the fate of the Domestic Help Act enacted after World War II as an overdue piece of labour protective legislation for domestic help, with limitations upon freedom of contract through unwaivable limits on working hours, overtime, etc. The preparation of the act prompted great debate, and the act was considered detailed and explicit enough to be of significant usefulnes for those it concerned. It was originally even recommended that the act be so simply worded that it could be easily read and understood by domestic helpers and used directly against employers. However, comprehensive studies on the Domestic Help Act established that the law had been used only to a small extent, and neither by housewives nor by their domestic help (Aubert et al. 1952, the Committee on the Domestic Help Act 1960). Such non-use by the very individuals the law sought to protect is of interest in understanding the relationship between law and society. But such an empirical finding can also have relevance for the interpretation of law. The use of passivity as a tool for interpreting legal rules is a classical theme in law, one that I will not dwell upon here.

Another example of women not being able to or not wanting to take advantage of their legal rights is provided in a rather large study of the application of the relatively new Swedish rules on more extensive rights in connection with pregnancy, childbirth and childcare. Surprisingly few women wanted to be away from their jobs for the entire period permitted by law. This was to some extent because the return to work became difficult in various respects if they utilized their right to paid leave to the full extent, but also because their working relationship with colleagues could deteriorate in the event that only inadequate temporary help was engaged (Widerberg 1984, Callemann et al. 1984). Even such an important women's reform as this is not necessarily utilized by those who were meant to benefit.

A Norwegian study of the allocation of the family home in divorce cases indicates that women tend to waive their rights —either because they do not realize how strong their position is in the settlement negotiation (practice dictates that the spouse awarded custody of the child or children also has the right to reside in the family home, in some cases even when the home is owned as separate property by the other spouse)—or because for various reasons they do not wish to insist on their rights. Women more than men often seem to live in 'two legal universes'—the technically correct and the real world (Vogt 1981).

An important element in modern interpretation of law is policy, i.e., whether a result appears expedient, reasonable and/ or just. The text of statutes and legislative history are objective facts to be construed, while policy to a large extent depends upon the interpreter's subjective beliefs and values. This can be a matter of taking into account what is accepted among lawyers or more generally in society, or what is in the process of becoming accepted. The direction of change in society's values is thus an element to be considered. In a society such as Norway, with a rather high degree of common values as compared to the situation in many other countries, there are in a way more objective possibilities of establishing which opinions and values are more or less accepted. To draw conclusions as to the nature and direction of these common values, the doctrinal writer relies first and foremost upon his own judgement.

The lawyer's judgement can be said to have two components —the generic and the subjective. The generic is acquired through a methodical and substantive study of law in a large number of fields, from which is derived the power of judgement when unsettled legal issues shall be resolved, and the better the schooling, the better the discernment. The other component is the more subjective common sense. This is, of course, also marked by one's general educational experience, but common sense at the same time contains ideological preferences and influences of a psychological and social character.

Common sense has played a significant role in legal doctrine, and good judgement is, of course, an essential legal guarantee. But if one were to take a critical view, one would realize that subjective common sense is quite often a tag attached to a result rather than a guide in the resolution of conflicts, except for such guidance as is given when legislation and legal theory empower those who apply the law to rely more or less upon their own discretion. To what extent this happens depends upon how willing those applying the law are to be influenced by policy. This policy is in the end nothing more than what those applying the law believe leads to a reasonable result, in the sense that the result in the specific case in question is either expedient or just. It is quite another matter to apply the same criteria in the interpretation and understanding of law in general. In such a case, generic judgement and subjective preferences, common sense and opinions of what is reasonable, expedient or just, all play important roles.

The difficult question then is where is the borderline between permissible and impermissible policy considerations with respect to the common values one must build upon within existing law. Individual and restricted group-centred policy that conflicts with cultural tradition and legal tradition raises the question how independent or critical those applying the law can permit themselves to be. Emphasizing women-centred policy considerations would in many situations probably not conflict with cultural tradition, such as it is in the real world, but *would* conflict with legal tradition. This means that it would, to begin with, be difficult to give much weight to them in the application of law, while—as will appear from chapter 5—they are of central importance in theory construction and legal politics. In time one must suppose that women-centred policy considerations will also prevail in terms of their use in the application of law, both in areas where they are expressly relied upon and in other areas where they are a part of the more general ideological development of society. In this respect, research in women's law has in my opinion, much to contribute to general legal science so that it may achieve a more realistic anchoring in the existing concrete qualities of society.

In every case it is essential to distinguish between the various tasks one embarks upon. If the task is to raise concrete legal questions and give concrete answers, as judges do, a legalistic approach to the law would be the fundamental first step. Individual decisions should, in my opinion, build upon a positivistic basic approach with relatively narrow limits on the use of policy. Extensive use of policy in individual cases raises problems with individual rights and liberties.

Administrative agencies are, of course, bound by their own interpretations of law, but often exercise discretion with great liberty. They should therefore—as discussed in section 4.5—be checked in various ways, and the law has special duties in that regard. The administrative decision must not only guarantee that like cases are treated like those treated in the past. It should especially strive for what is useful, appropriate and just with respect to the present and future. It is therefore both necessary and desirable that administrative agencies should be flexible in the exercise of discretion. The question is to what extent and under what conditions the authorities are or ought to be entitled to change course with the idea of a more effective future in mind.

It is quite a different matter when the legal task is concerned with what legal scholars do with the aim of understanding and later acting in relation to other rules and possible consequences in the future. A 'free law' method and reasoning ought to be applicable in such a situation, both in theory construction and legal politics—of course with due care for the general requirements of science.

This difference in attitude toward legal positivism, depending upon whether one is faced with individual decisions or scientific analysis, is, in my opinion, not emphasized often enough.

The systemization of norms (science, rule formation, and legal politics) and the practical interpretation of norms (the application of law) are two very different types of activity. When legal theory and proposals for rule formation and other legal politics are concerned, lawyers are free to assert their fundamental values. It is the *quality* of the use of method and the reasoning behind the assertion and proposals which determine what is good or bad, not whether the assertions and proposals are defensible within the framework of existing law. When the concrete application of law is concerned, it is quite a different matter. In such a case objections can be raised against the 'free law' approach which today predominates with respect to the use of legal sources both in practice and in legal science. For weak groups and the opponents of status quo society there is essential value in an application of rule-of-law principles such as predictability and individual rights and liberty, even though one might have achieved better results in specific individual cases with the application of a 'free law' method. In other cases the interest of the strong and the keepers of the status quo could succeed on the basis of a 'free law' theory. It is therefore not in the interest of women's law to stretch the law and predictability too far in order to reach a victory in a specific fact situation. That same victory could prove to be short-lived and even increase the likelihood of concrete losses in other situations by helping to entrench a general 'free law' method.

As pointed out earlier, women's law, at least as it is conducted at the University of Oslo today, concentrates more on theory, general interpretation of law and legal politics than on the interpretation of law and application of law in concrete fact situations.

However, the opportunity to address women's law problems on the basis of the solution of individual controversies does exist, namely through the use of the organization 'Legal Aid for Women' as well as through women lawyers. Their role is not that of legal theorist or decision-maker, but that of counsel and representative. And an advocate must be permitted to go far in the argument of policy. For the advocate it is a question of what is strategically best for the client. In a concrete controversy she must be allowed to benefit from the fact that the sources of law theory is as flexible and open as it is today, and to try to convince the judge or civil servant to decide in favour of her client. It is the duty of those who apply the law to set limits as to its application. Civil and criminal procedure is so thoroughly balanced that the attorneys for the parties need not feel restricted to a sources of law theory that one believes ought to exist when the client can benefit from that which exists here and now. In this sense the advocate, in opposition to the legal theorist and judge, can be opportunistic and strategic in the concrete case.

In a discussion of 'free law' approaches or positivistic approaches to law, one must distinguish between giving weight to policy and giving weight to the general public opinion of what the law is or ought to be. Such general public opinion is a phenomenon which can at least be identified in a more certain way than what can be described as an expedient or just result based on the opinion of the person applying the law. With its empirical foundation, the general public opinion of what law is or ought to be approaches custom as a source of law more than policy does. Opinions about general social development and the general public opinion of what law is or ought to be, are often a part of the legal reasoning behind the use of policy considerations, their content and weight. At the same time, such legal reasoning gives an illusion of a united public opinion. However, the differences in the sexes in the real world must also be presumed to be reflected in the opinions of the two sexes about law and justice. In one area such sex-divided opinions of the law have recently been documented, namely concerning legal protection against pornography. The reaction to 'United Action Against Pornography and Prostitution' seems to reveal widespread differences between women and men as to opinions of what the law ought to be. The Criminal Law Advisory Council took account of this sex-based dichotomy both in its description and evaluation of the development of existing law (see p. 47).

Legal science that incorporates empirical differences between the sexes concerning opinions of what the law is or ought to be, or that describes special women-centred policy considerations to be given weight, will gradually obtain greater support in law reform, legal theory and in practice. Women-centred policy considerations will thus become a part of the general legal tradition. Legal science outside women's law would, in my opinion, also have something to gain here, so as to render their disciplines more holistic and more realistically anchored. Let me therefore elaborate at greater length on the nature and weight of these considerations.

5

Policy Considerations

Women-centred policy considerations are the *values* that are accorded special weight in women's law. These values—ideals of 'the good society'—are essential, both in the evaluation of existing law, and as criteria for the structure and methodology of women's law, and even as indicators of reform ideals. The values are thus used analytically to give substance to the expression 'women's law', born of the intention to describe, explain and understand women's legal position. Moreover, they give insight into how women's position can be improved, in law and in society. There is thus a continual interaction of the different elements in the definition; the women-centred policy considerations of women's law run through them and bind them together.

What considerations are being referred to, and what material content are they ascribed in different contexts?

We seek first the long-term, more or less absolute considerations and interests that set the tone for women's law's systematics and moral critique of existing law, so as to identify the basic values women's law is built upon.

5.1. Basic Values. Law and Morals

The primary considerations I begin with are justice and freedom. Within these, other sets of values are found, first and foremost, equality, dignity, integrity, self-determination, and self-realization.

Justice and freedom are of course fundamental principles in legal theory generally. In the abstract there would hardly be any disagreement that these considerations ought to be accorded weight, but there is widespread disagreement as to what that specifically entails and about the priority to be given. This section will discuss justice and freedom generally. The sections that follow will give specific examples of their uses in concrete applications of law, in systematic and controversial questions of legal politics.

The concepts justice and freedom convey notions that are easy to accept. Consequently they may at first glance appear meaningless and nondescript, except for the importance attached to the recognition of values as fundamental for the workings of an academic discipline. In connection with research this is neither unique nor unusual, though women's law perhaps goes further, attaching greater significance to the identification of its fundamental values and the examination of their substance and usefulness.

General and comprehensive values like justice and freedom are often used to obtain support in political affairs. Thus some warn against the use of such concepts in research. The contents of the notions are said to be so varied, imprecise, emotionally charged, and moreover so difficult to test empirically that they mask and mislead rather than reveal and clarify. The historian Jens Arup Seip, whose historical writings are especially 'revealing', has recently criticized the multifarious use of the Norwegian concept 'rettsstat', 'the rule of law'. While referring to the fact that at least 161 scientific works in post-war German law have dealt with this concept, he warns against it, and asserts that the concept of 'the rule of law' confounds the present Norwegian debate (Seip 1984). The analysis of the different and contradictory meanings of concepts is of course an important research task. Rather than warn against its use, I would assert that the preoccupation of researchers of an entire generation with the concept of 'the rule of law' in itself makes it especially interesting and appropriate as a subject for research and debate. The fact is that the concept attracts special interest; and is therefore a well-suited gathering point for different approaches and uses, in this case, scientific and governmental competition over the meaning of precisely a concept so many hold in esteem. The circumstances allow for such competition and with that, the articulation of different interest groups, fulfilling a necessary condition not only for democracy, but also for peaceful social change.

Considerations of value questions in the end always depend on moral choice. The relationship between law and morality is an old theme, but in my opinion a theme too peripheral for far too long. In order to place the ideals of women's law in a proper context, it may be useful to take a retrospective glance at this theme in Norwegian legal history.

Under the influence of natural science's methods and the arrival of empirical social sciences in the nineteenth century, the belief in objective science thrust its way into the world of norms as well. Anton Martin Schweigaard—the founding father of Norwegian jurisprudence—argued for the greatest possible use of pure empiricism in order to understand society and thus govern it through law. He wanted to gather all possible material on fundamental social conditions and to analyze it by using legal, socio-economic and statistical methods in holistic social science in which law too was integrated (Sandvik 1985). Schweigaard's positivistic ideal, together with his talent for the practical and useful, paved the way for the pragmatic legal realism typical of Norwegian law until today. Legal positivism and utilitarianism rule today at the expense of moral philosophy and a broad spectrum of policy ideals. Belief in objectivity and scientific neutrality has pushed aside interest in the legal order's built-in ethical assessment and moral critique. Of course, one man cannot be given the credit for 150 years of historical development. But it is striking how forcefully the ideas of natural law have been repudiated in Norway, how meagre the debate on legal and moral philosophy has been, and how far legal pragmatism has penetrated at the expense of generalizing theory and concept formation. "Conceptualism", like natural law, now casts a long shadow of distrust and disbelief (Anners 1983: 352, Skirbekk 1985, Castberg 1975).

The future of moral philosophy was particularly grim under the oppressive influence of the Uppsala philosophy with its utilitarian anchoring. Yet even the emphasis on utility and effectiveness involves a moral choice. But its morality was, in my opinion, distortedly one-sided. The distinctive Scandinavian realism that characterized legal philosophy in post-war Scandinavia until far into the 1960s was also to a large degree coloured by this one-sidedness. It argued that law should be a science of existing law, a reality *sui generis*. The focal point of this philosophy was the so-called prediction theory, with Alf Ross as its principal theoretician. Legal pronouncements of existing law were to serve as the empirical basis for the most objective prediction possible of judicial conduct based on a hypothetical-deductive method, patterned after natural science and the empirical social sciences. A realistic formulation of legal sources theory and existing law theory were to be built upon what courts could be expected to do, not upon what they were 'obliged' to do. Ross generally distanced himself from all concepts with normative contents; he asserted in an early work that they must 'be considered the same as a scream or a cry of hurrah: neither of them signify any existing thing, but all can be understood as spontaneous expressions of an immediate subjective experience, a gush of emotion or impulse.' (Ross 1940: cf. Castberg 1975:320).

Furthermore, in his later influential book 'On Law and Justice' Ross rejected claims of material justice with the statement that 'invoking justice is the same as banging on the table: an emotional expression which transforms one's demand into an absolute postulate and that's that' (Ross 1953:358). In similar fashion Ross at various times sharply criticized natural law philosophers, without giving a sufficiently impartial rendition of their theories (see for example Ross 1963).

The trend reversed in the 1970s. The interest in normative-political theory saw an international renaissance thrusting considerations of 'justice' into the spotlight again, with John Rawls' pioneer work 'A Theory of Justice' (1971). The same year Torstein Eckhoff published his major treatise 'Justice' (Eckhoff 1971).

In addition, the 'critical law' movement arrived in Norway—a by-product of general academic criticism in Europe after 1968. Legal practitioners and social science researchers to a greater degree than before brought their professions into the political arena by siding explicitly with rejected and weak groups. In Norwegian social science research (which has always had strong ties to law and legal issues) political engagement was a tradition throughout the 1960s. By their research and participation in public affairs alike, university professors like Vilhelm Aubert, Nils Christie, Yngvar Løchen, Thomas Mathiesen and Odd Steffen Dalgard left their mark on the debates of social and criminal policy. Internationally, this engagement was further stimulated and politicized, with students and researchers taking part in increasing numbers.

As early as 1968 ex-convicts, criminologists, lawyers and sociologists founded the 'Norwegian Society for Criminal Reform' (KROM) for the immediate improvement of prison conditions and for short-term and long-term criminal-policy objectives. With the help of theoretical insight, practical work began, stimulating programs for action theory (Mathiesen 1971) and different types of action-oriented research. The ideal of interaction between theory and practice also characterized the establishment of the law student clinic (Juss-Buss) in 1972, Legal Advice for Women (JURK) in the Spring of 1974, the Law and Politics Society and the Journal of Critical Law in the autumn of 1974.

All of these practical initiatives (and others) had their origin in the law faculty milieu at the University of Oslo. Together with the larger movements of academic criticism in universities across Europe they have had great influence on the general academic theory development of the 1970s, as well as on the growing academic specialty fields, such as social security law, women's law and children's law. The legal philosopher Nils Kristian Sundby led the theoretical work; and under the influence of the group publishing the German journal *Kritische Justiz* and the Frankfurt School, the critical law movement proposed a reassessment of law and the legal system in the light of moral and political values (Sundby 1974 b and 1975, Bratholm and Sundby (eds.) 1976).

5.2. Justice

Justice must be considered a basic legal norm, thus belonging to the concept of law itself. Its fundamental place has at times been more intuitively understood than directly analyzed in law. 'Never has the [Norwegian] Supreme Court been forced by a law to render a judgment it considered unjust'—a Supreme Court justice once declared during court proceedings, without anyone reacting except for Fredrik Stang, a law professor temporarily designated a substitute judge (Stang 1942:19).

According to a distinction introduced by Eckhoff, justice

can be understood as a value which appears in two types of relationships: equivalent justice[1] and distributive justice. Equivalent justice applies to situations where two parties exchange benefits or evils with each other. Examples are barter and sale, or the division of work and money between spouses based on an assessment of each spouse's contribution or effort. One can also evaluate the position of recipients of social security on the basis of equivalent justice: Is it reasonable that social security benefits are based on the insured's effort as reflected in earned income and social security tax paid (insurance principle), or should the insured be granted a minimum sum regardless of the amount of tax paid in? We see in this example how equivalent justice can serve as one of the criteria in the evaluation of distributive justice. Compensation for negligent and intentional torts; payment given and payment received in commercial law; all kinds of terms of trade between two parties, both in and out of the marketplace—all of these can be subjected to the same test of a just equivalence. In criminal law one can discuss whether the crime is proportionate to the punishment—an eye for an eye? Or just a tooth for a tooth?

Distributive justice covers, on the other hand, situations where the benefits and evils are distributed among a given number of recipients. The distribution can be based on an equal result: equal quantities to each, independent of need, or even of effort; or equal rations of scarce resources. Proportional equality is also conceivable, the standard of measure being effort, need, result or potential. Justice in distribution can involve the establishment of a ranking system, for example the queue principle: first come, first served. It can involve a just distribution, not of the benefits themselves, but of the chance of acquiring them—an equality of chance, for example in the drawing of lots.

Considerations of justice are always present in the application of law; they come under the category 'policy considerations', which was discussed earlier (see section 4.6). 'Like cases' should be treated alike, or at least the differences created should not

---

1. Eckhoff's concept is sometimes translated by the term 'retributive justice'. However, because Eckhoff used the term to encompass some types of reciprocity in relations between parties (e.g. purchase and sale) which do not include retribution. I have chosen to use the term 'equivalent justice'.

be contrary to what 'policy considerations' dictate. There are, of course, differences of opinion as to what is a 'like case', depending upon whether it is determined by 'like efforts', 'like results', or 'like needs'. 'Equal pay for work of equal value' is a principle whose interpretation embodies such disagreement—the official view having enormous practical consequences for women (Halvorsen 1985 a). A consideration of justice often found in the application of law is typified by the rule that all who fulfil the requirements relating to X or to Y ought to have an equal chance to compete under an arrangement for equal competition. The chapters that follow will give many examples of evaluations of equality, their variations and significance.

The requirement of justice plays a role as a women-centred policy consideration wherever the objective is to reach a reasonable and appropriate result in the application of law. Whether it concerns the distribution of benefits and evils between the two sexes in or outside the marketplace, or between the two parties in marriage, justice is a material consideration. The importance of this value, however, stretches far beyond the simple application of law. The division into legal categories such as housewives' law (see chapter 7), money law (chapter 6) and paid-work law (chapter 8) are simply reflections from various perspectives of law viewed through a superior prism of justice, crystallized by numerous inequitable divisions which together constitute women's unjustly weak position in law and society.

Within the logical order of women's law this legal categorization is not, however, grounded from above like an axiomatic application of the superior principle of justice. Admittedly, many philosophers have argued that especially ethics, the choice of moral values, must be grounded from above, out of general principles of an axiomatic character which in turn guarantee correct applications to the extent that the axioms themselves are correct. However, there are also theories proposed which assert that ethics can be grounded from below, patterned on the hypothetical-deductive method. Rawls advances such a theory in justifying his concept of justice.

Rawls believes that we must start with all the various individual ethical beliefs we have in different areas, and then formulate general moral principles from which the individual ethical beliefs emanate (Rawls 1983:577 f, Føllesdal et al. 1983:100–101).

Considerations of justice in women's law start by identifying the needs and wants of women in general, and particularly their opinions about what is just. Out of this matrix of needs and opinions we may develop a series of hypotheses about values on the basis of which we wish to study and examine the law. We then allow the individual legal rules and sets of rules to confront these values and the principles derived from these values. This provides a foundation for new hypotheses about the compatibility or incompatibility of the legal rules and the derived principles, which are then tested, on the basis of our own experiences and women's presumed needs, wants and notions of justice.

Research on the conditions under which women live seems to indicate that there are principally three areas where women experience unjust distribution: money, time, and work. This uneven distribution of the three valuables—money, time, and work—has provided a basis for systematizing three areas of women's law: money law, housewives' law, and paid-work law.

The right to one's own money is an explicit need for women. A minimum amount of one's own money is a minimum welfare requirement in a money economy. The 'money law' perspective of legal rules results from society's unjust distribution of the flow of cash. There are large systematic differences between women's and men's access to money, and the differences cannot be said to be ethically justified, either with respect to equivalent justice or to distributive justice. The systematic structure of social security law and tax law provides many examples of such systematic differences (Sverdrup 1984 b and 1985). This applies to the systematic structure of tort law as well (Kjønstad 1984 a, Bull 1985).

In marriage, equality between woman and man is problematic from a money-law perspective, principally because care of the house and family earns no economic payment. The wife has no right to an equal share of the family income, and no right to the husband's money other than a certain amount of household money and a certain amount for herself. If the husband earns a lot of money, for example, because the wife bears the entire responsibility of care for house and family, the husband can simply keep the money for himself. She has no right to pension points of her own and no right to share his;[2] either arrangement would be 'equivalently just', if work in the home and work outside the home were valued equally (Hellum 1985). If such equivalent justice were a reality and one were to assess statistically the value of care of family or household on the basis of 'effort', the resulting graph would show extreme variations among women with respect to economic yield, since the yield would be dependent upon how prosperous one's husband was.

Based on distributive justice, however, one could propose the introduction of a minimum standard, a minimum amount of money to all adults over a certain age regardless of need. The main point is that a minimum amount of money for oneself is a necessary prerequisite for personal freedom, self-determination and self-realization—values I will discuss in the next section.

The extent of caretaking work required, and the inter-dependency between all parties involved in caretaking, result in women generally having less free time than men (Fastvold 1985). Work outside the home can also lead to time constriction, but such working hours have limits and are subject to extensive regulation. But when care is required for children, the elderly or the sick, the caretaker's hours are not regulated. The caretaker simply cannot fail when duty calls. There are scarcely any arrangements to relieve the caretaker and no valuation in money or pension points. The life of a caretaker—say, a housewife—for long periods is characterized by scarcity of free time—and most women are housewives, either full-time, part-time or overtime. A more equal distribution of time in the family and in the marketplace is, inter alia, one of the considerations of justice which forms the basis for the legal discipline called 'housewives' law'.

What then should be divided—the work or the valuation of it? Much of the moral atmosphere around the demand for equality in today's society might indicate that women want a total sharing of all duties in marriage. However, the women interviewed for the women's law project 'Division of Money and Community Property' (Hellum and Fastvold 1985) were not so concerned about total sharing as they were about the

2. Pension points are points accumulated on the basis of the size of one's pensionable income. It is the accumulation of pension points that entitles an insured person to a pension in excess of the basic (minimum) pension.

desire to obtain greater justice in the valuation of their work, inter alia, as caretakers in the home. Government (state) valuation in terms of money and clearer rights regarding division of both spouses' income and pension points are thus objectives both in 'money law' and housewives' law.

But the distribution of work in society also raises questions of justice. There are conspicuous differences between women's and men's opportunities in employment, i.e., in obtaining employment, staying employed, and enjoying a fixed salary (Halvorsen 1985 a and b, see also chapter 8 below). Women are short-changed without ethical justification in *all* categories of work distribution and in the dispensation of rewards. 'Paid-work law' systematizes the legal significance of this discrimination. The term indicates moreover that the concept of work in women's law encompasses more than income-producing work, and that in our opinion considerations of justice require an essential societal re-evaluation of care of the household and family.

The three legal disciplines—money law, housewives' law, and paid-work law—each constitute a separate entity. The individual opinions and hypotheses combine with the principle demanding a more equitable division of money, time and work, to form one perspective. Allowing considerations of justice to serve as the systematizing criterium, money law addresses rules whose effect is to deny women their own source of money, while housewives' law deals with rules for the care of household and family and all that concerns women as part-time or full-time housewives. Paid-work law examines the unjust legal position of women in the marketplace, inequities completely lacking ethical justification.

In addition to functioning as a principle in the application of law and begetting the structure of women's law with its moral grounding from below, considerations of justice plot the course of legal reforms proposed in women's law.

Thus far, work in the area of women's law has formed the intellectual basis for several new proposals for reforms and has prompted alternative routines and procedures in government policy in Norway. Some of these are explicitly outlined in this book. Furthermore, gender-based demands for justice also raise important questions about the distribution of benefits and evils in society generally. To the extent that the reforms are meant to promote welfare, the question arises how one grounds the desire to distribute such welfare. There are several theoretical possibilities.

Some believe that it is the individual's welfare, i.e., that individual evaluation is the important starting point; see, for example, Richard Posner's ideology in *Law and Economics* (Posner 1977). Others prefer a minimum standard for everyone. Still others would require special criteria as the basis for distribution. According to Rawls, reforms that distribute unequally are just only when they distribute in such a way that those who are 'worse-off' are better off than they would have been had the distribution been more equal (Rawls 1983:303). Safeguarding the worse-off is an attractive goal. But Rawls presumes that man is willing to tolerate great disparity so that the worse-off will be better off or at least not worse off, while simultaneously accepting that the rich get richer.

One women's law proposal, for example, is minimum wages for everyone. To what should this minimum wage correspond? It is a fact that the worse-off have the lowest possible standard of living, but there would be little satisfaction if reforms only effected an adjustment to this standard. The minimum pension should perhaps be the starting point for normalizing a minimum standard for everyone, despite the fact that it would necessitate that the social security principle of 'accustomed standard of living' be considerably modified for some groups.[3] One should thus start with the National Insurance Act's 'basic amount',[4] its special supplement *(særtillegg)* and compensation supplement *(kompensasjonstillegg)*, i.e., NOK 40,000 per year (as of 1987), as a rough estimate in the effort to establish a minimum right to money.

Another objection to Rawls' point of view is that there would be broad disagreement about who is worse off. Is it the wife who with her family lives on the poverty line, but whose family

3. Social security's built-in principle of 'accustomed standard of living' means that an insured with a greater income will, for many benefits, be entitled to a correspondingly greater benefit.
4. The 'basic amount' is the index-linked standard amount for all social security calculations according to the National Insurance Act. As per 1 May 1980 the annual basic amount was NOK 16,900 (£1336). See chapter 7, p. 5.

functions harmoniously with both spouses sharing everything, —or is it the wife who through her husband's prosperity lives in abundance, but without access to her own money, merely receiving payment in kind authorized by her husband? When human dignity and integrity are considered as well as the right to dispose of one's own money, it could be questionable who was worse off. The same is true when considered from a money-law perspective.

Furthermore, even if one succeeded in identifying the worse-off, the distribution of benefits and evils creates many problems, because the performers in the distribution drama may have very different interests. As seen from the point of view of the weakest party, some aspects of reform might be good, others bad, without the tilting of the balance being evident.

For example, paternalistic legislation for the protection of women can be good, born of intentions to protect weak parties, and be designed to promote a more just distribution. But from women's perspective these laws can at the same time prove repugnant, because they operate discriminatorily in that they restrict women's freedom and right to self-determination. An illustrative example is the stormy debate at the turn of the century about the introduction of special protective legislation for women working in industry. Some advocated such legislation to protect women's reproductive function. They wanted to defend her integrity and health by restricting employers' use of women in certain work situations: night work, shift work, especially heavy or polluted jobs, etc. Others promoted the same legislation for ulterior motives. Trade unions (only men) advocated special protective legislation because it was in their interest to shut women out of the competition for jobs. In certain enterprises employers were especially disposed to using female labour because it was cheaper, a factor that in the trade union's view both contributed to the depression of salaries, and to the employment of women at the expense of men. Women themselves were deeply divided on the point. Some considered protective legislation a false paternalism, rules designed to make competition with men more difficult, while others regarded the legislation as reforms, properly directed to favouring women's duties of childbirth and child care. The question of how one should place 'the weakest' in the best possible position, involves choosing which existing or potential factors have contributed (or are contributing) to the weak position of women: women's duty of childbirth, their opportunities to enter the job market, the terms on which they are employed, or their competition as employees in relationship to others. Whichever factors are choosen, those are the factors to be improved upon. It is a task of women's law to identify the empirical factors involved in such questions. The vast majority of work performed by women today is done at inconvenient times. Because of employer needs, the availability of women, and the transition to the two-income family model, women take work that complements men's normal work hours—shift work, night work, work situations where the Working Environment Act's principal rules seldom apply and normal working days seldom occur. All in all the new working and family habits of today have led to Scandinavian women in the cities working comparatively more, and under comparatively harder conditions than before (Widerberg 1980, Nielsen 1979, Rødsets and Titlestad 1984). In the countryside the pattern might be somewhat different; women farmers of the previous generation had much harder and heavier work than they do today.

The difficulties concerning legal reforms to improve women's position do not just lie in the identification of the 'worse-off' or the aspects of their situation which can effectively be improved. It is also difficult to foresee the consequences of the equalizing measures being proposed. It requires enormous resources to take on such rational and scientific planning. Research in women studies has few resources. When, based on the fundamental value of justice, we propose a more equitable distribution of money, time, and work, we must do this out of faith in our fundamental distribution principle, without being required to give an account in full detail of all the possible consequences of such distribution, as well as to declare where the money is to be taken from. This would be unjust, since women's law researchers seldom have the same research and design capacity as more organized interest groups in our corporative structure. The burden should be on politicians and other authorities, on the basis of fundamental values underlying stated wants and needs, to earmark resources so that weak groups can articulate themselves. The investigation of proposed legislation that weak groups constantly request, or research where one perhaps does not know the nature of the benefits to be reaped, has in my estimation a good foundation in prevailing notions of democracy and the decision-making process, where one engages also in the examination of more or less well-grounded considerations and gives them meaning as normatively decisive for action. Modern decision theory makes greater allowance for this than classical utilitarianism (Føllesdal et al. 1983:241 f). According to decision theory, it is sensible to act upon the little we know or believe, rather than act blindly.

Women's law as an academic discipline is only 10–15 years old. It lacks a schedule of arguments and evaluation patterns pro and con as well ordered and worked out in as rich detail, as other established disciplines, where legal considerations have had both time and resources to draw from. This is mentioned as a concluding consideration of justice before I turn to the other primary consideration in women's law: Freedom.

5.3. Freedom

Freedom is the fundamental notion in natural law; and ideas of natural law were of primary importance in the national patriotic unity around 1814 when Norway became a sovereign country. Later the Constitution stood there as an existing fact of natural law, and Frederik Stang's 1833 analysis of the Constitution was the first legal work in the new Norway in which an entire legal discipline was expounded on the basis of rules of positive law.

Freedom is a basic value in both constitutional law and international law. It serves to point the way in the shaping of rights and duties of individuals and states. It is the protection of the individual's freedom that will be discussed here, especially its relevance for the position of women. I will not go into the substance of civil and political rights of individuals according to existing law; rather, using the concept of freedom as a point of departure, I seek to deduce the ethical components in the evaluation of protected rights that are most relevant for women.

I have discussed above the social and economic rights, using the concept of justice, and in this are incorporated ethical principles of distribution based on equality and equal worth. If these principles of distribution are implemented to a greater extent than they are today, that in itself is an achievement. But the *result* of a more just distribution is also a means to bring us closer to the ideals of freedom. A more even distribution of the right to one's own money and time, and a more equal valuation of different types of work, are essential prerequisites to lay the foundation for the individual's freedom of action and expression. The distribution system today contains a host of barriers to the participation of women, i.e., self-determination and joint decision-making in community life. When these barriers are taken down, the oppression of women will diminish. Thus, through the politics of equality and equal merit, a foundation can be laid for liberation—the ultimate ideal in the objective of freedom.

Just as the concept 'justice', as a goal for the future, has injustice as its negation in the existing state of things, the concept 'freedom' has its negation in restraint, force, and dependency. The application of the concept 'freedom' in women's law must therefore discuss the assault on and encroachment upon women's freedom. The protection of values such as dignity and integrity are essential in this connection. Through such protection the foundation is built for self-determination and self-realization.

That these considerations are identified as of principal importance to women's law does not mean that they are limited to the sphere of women. They involve general considerations anchored in ideas of human rights. This means that the freedom of certain individuals is often gained at the expense of the freedom of other individuals, just as certain groups in society do not merely have greater freedom than other groups, but have it at the expense of other groups. Viewed from this perspective, women's dependence upon men is a moral problem, both on an individual and a societal level.

Just as one must find a just balance in the distribution of scarce resources, one must seek the realization of a well-considered balance between the individual choices of various forms of life, life styles, and different roads to self-realization. In the search for this well-considered balance, it is thus not just a question of individual freedom so highly prized among liberal values, but also a question of the search for principles of collec-

tive self-realization, i.e., self-realization in working for and together with others. Just as the individual right to self-determination is limited by other persons and other groups' joint decision-making and self-determination, the more fundamental
choices of one's path in life and the expression of one's creative
force must also be assessed in relationship to others and together
with others.

The anchoring of values must also in this context be grounded
from below, not from above. The foundation must be shaped
from women's expressed and presumed needs and wants; it
must be measured against the legal order's regulation of the
same circumstances and aligned with general principles which
we deduce from this interplay of concrete experiences and ethical principles.

In the following I shall render a more precise explanation of
the essence of the concept 'freedom' based on this interplay of
morality and women's experience.

Dignity and Integrity
Dignity and personal integrity are the fundamental elements of
human self-esteem and self-respect.

Dignity is connected to the need for acknowledgement of
one's personal and/or group qualities, distinguishable characteristics and special activities. It involves first and foremost one's
own valuation, i.e. valuation on one's own premises, preferably
supported by one's immediate surroundings, but not necessarily
by many. One can also speak of dignity of a more societal or
public nature based on outer criteria such as rank, age, etc.

An example of how the official notions of dignity are reflected
in the law is given by Gjelsvik and Dons Wankel in their critical
analysis of social security benefits to 'surviving spouses and
other widows'. They concluded that both the conditions for and
the rules regulating the amount of allowance are reflected in
a social hierarchy—'a scale of dignity'—which evaluates the
survivor according to a series of criteria such as cohabitation,
care and maintenance relationship, cause of death, the reason
for the husband's disappearance or absence, etc., as opposed to
being based on the *need* for support (Gjelsvik and Wankel 1980).
Another example outlines the rules for assessing compensation
on the death of a housewife, in comparison with compensation

on the death of a wage-earning husband. While the housewife's work is assessed lowly while she is living, it can become valuable at her death. At that point her efforts become tangible in that the husband's need becomes prominent. The reverse situation can arise when he dies and she becomes eligible for compensation. While he was alive his work was assessed according to his efforts. At his death it is the amount of the housewife's loss which is to be compensated, and it is generally assessed lowly (Kjønstad 1984 a).

Legal conclusions of this kind are not merely expressions of a general valuation of different types of work effort and needs, but also they *reinforce* such valuations and leave their marks on individual lives. There is a continual interaction between official patterns of assessment and the more or less private notions of dignity as seen from the individual's perspective. From this perspective below, the consideration of dignity is intimately connected to self-esteem and self-respect.

Through research in women's law, Fastvold and Hellum have shown the significant aspects of these notions concerning women's dignity and integrity as seen from a perspective below. In an examination of the practice of married couples concerning distribution of money, time, and work in the family, they found that considerations for dignity and integrity were most prominent among women (Hellum and Fastvold 1985). It isn't only important that one gets money. *How* one gets money for subsistence means a great deal for one's identity and dignity in a money economy. 'To feel that they receive money from their husbands, that it is their husbands' money, to have to ask for money, or to have to answer for the use of money, are for many serious threats to their dignity'. The women interviewed wanted to be treated with dignity, and this need was a general need that crossed all sectors of women's life, work and conflict situations. Dignity was one of the concerns expressed in the legislative history of the Marriage Act's rules which establish by law the right to household money and one's own money (Hellum 1985).

Dignity as an attribute is often treated in women studies, first and foremost as a strong characteristic in the more or less hidden women culture, which specifically emphasizes women's pride and dignity (Sørensen 1977:182 ff)—that 'women are okay, women experiences are important—and they are ours'

(Holter 1977:291) etc. In an interesting treatise of Frances Fox Piven the concept of dignity appears constantly when she compares women's situation and history with that of farmers. Just as farmers, women previously lived at the periphery of modern society's market and state, insulated and isolated in a barter economy, and on the sidelines of a money economy. A large literature of the history of farmers shows how they developed ideas and values that reflected their experiences in life. In a society where the barter economy was in decline, it was precisely the values of the home which were valued by farmers. In the same way women's self-awareness made them feel that their living function was to be natural providers. Women valued the family, celebrated motherhood and the care of children and husband; they honoured family ties that secured both themselves and their work. In other words women developed a traditional 'moral economy', a morality of care and an economy of care which, even though it was created in dependence on the patriarchal money economy, carried in itself pride and dignity in their own work efforts. The values of care of house and family gave women the power to counteract and change the dominating values of the public sector, especially in the market, both in the previous century and today, because the awareness of the enormous value of their care gave them dignity (Piven 1985:72 f).

This dignity has in periods of history been challenged and broken down by condescending notions of housework and housewives. Modern politics of equality, with its heavy emphasis on paid work, and on men's lives and life-style as the norm, has in many ways been both offensive and difficult for many women, both on the individual level—as the the legal investigation underscores—and in politics.

Development of the concepts birth law and housewives' law is an answer to this challenge. The concepts signal the necessity of gathering, evaluating and developing the fragmented rules which today regulate birth and caretaking work, and which through increased legal protection can support the values which this work represents.

The notion of integrity has a close connection with the notion of dignity, but it is especially connected to the right *to be left in peace*, both physically and psychologically. While dignity is aimed at self-respect and acknowledgement, at least from one's most immediate surroundings, integrity is actually 'the condition of being untouched'—a result of the individual's demand for protection against unwarranted encroachment or infringement from other persons or society. (When we say about a critic that he or she 'has integrity', the connotation is somewhat different, i.e., that the person in question judges objectively and on the merits).

Marianne Fastvold's description of housework emphasizes how the extent and type of work—the working and living conditions inherent in the demands for continuous care and confining proximity, the many duties, lack of relief etc.—can in themselves contain a serious threat to women's integrity. To what degree and in what way the women interviewed had experienced this seemed to be closely connected to the personal relationship existing between the spouses. If the woman was given her husband's interest, support and respect, she could tolerate a great deal and work hard, even if the husband had to be away much because of his job, for example on business travels etc. However, if the husband belonged to the group of uncooperative, controlling or even violent husbands, this was not only experienced as a series of difficult situations and isolated attacks, but as generally threatening to one's identity, self-respect and work capacity (Fastvold 1985).

In this way the women interviewed voiced the important distinction between structural (societal) and personal (private) oppression. If the relationships between the parties are good, women tolerate more of the objective difficulties with their life situation as wife, mother and housewife (Dahl 1976).

Protection against violations of integrity has been in the centre of women's politics the last few years, and women studies have contributed by revealing the nature and extent of these violations, analyzing their effects, and suggesting possible reforms.

Attention has been directed to offences that only women are exposed to. Wife-beating necessarily victimizes the physically weaker party, while rape, incest, pornography and prostitution represent sexual offences against and sexual profiteering primarily at the expense of women.

Across the entire western world there have sprung up since

the 1970s a host of action groups, contact organizations and support measures reaching from woman to woman in order to meet these violations that have gone on throughout time. The social energy in these initatives—almost all of them operated on a voluntary basis, from San Francisco to Helsinki—is noteworthy. It stands out as one of the conspicuous expressions of the capability of the new women's movement for quick and spontaneous action, with extensive use of the 'learn by imitation' method as a means to spread different initiatives across national boundaries with different social and legal systems.

The 1970s revelation of mistreatment of women—especially wife-beating—has given rise to an especially active 'crisis centre' movement in Norway today, with 35 centres and 21 crisis telephones spread over the entire country and in about as many municipalities.

The sale of pornographic magazines and videofilms has been kept under the scrutiny of a large number of interested action groups, which in only a short time have had some success in the demand for legislative reform.

Programs of action research involving prostitution in the larger cities in Norway have attracted much public attention with their real life observations, encounters and profound empathy with the very young girls that are forced into the streets, often because of drug abuse.

Work with rape victims has first and foremost concerned itself with the improvement of the victim's humiliating position in the criminal law process, where they often experience the encounter with police and courts as a new source of humiliation. Feminist lawyers sought to avoid this 'double rape' through proposed reforms in the criminal law process. The work proved fruitful, with changes in the Criminal Procedure Act in 1981, which gave rape victims the right to legal assistance at the cost of the state (see the Criminal Procedure Act sections 113–116). Setting limits to the court's right to hear evidence of the victim's previous conduct and sexual experience has been emphasized as well. As for incest victims, they have received support primarily as a result of an increased understanding that health personnel today show toward this problem, which along with wife abuse and rape is now thought to be far more widespread than was earlier presumed.

In the last few years the question of what criminal law responses could most effectively deter sexual offences has aroused considerable debate. Researchers in women's law have in this context relied upon the general conviction in criminology and criminal law that increased punishment seldom leads to a change in conduct in an area like this—and that a change in conduct must despite everything be the main objective. For rape victims the legal system will seldom involve restitution. It is doubtful whether more frequent reporting of rape will help those who are victimized, even though a more active reporting practice can have political meaning and influence general attitudes. A rape victim can receive a certain economic compensation from the state upon reporting the offence. But she also risks that the accused will be acquitted because of certain legal presumptions—especially when it concerns satisfaction of the subjective requirements for conviction combined with the important legal presumption that any reasonable doubt is resolved in favour of the accused. This means that it is the man's credibility that to a large extent is determinative, with the consequence for the woman that she is further degraded and victimized.

A similar contradiction would arise if a prostitute were forced to testify in criminal proceedings against the paying customer if the demand for the criminalization of his activity should succeed. To the extent that one wants to support the victims of prostitution—the prostitutes—the demand for prosecution of the customers will most likely work against one's intention.

In the pornography debate the demand for increased prohibition raises the question of how far in the direction of 'soft' pornography such a prohibition should probably go. In the recent amendment to section 211 of the Criminal Code this decision is left entirely to the discretion of the judge without more detailed guidance in the legislative history. The border that one must necessarily set qualitatively hardly affects what many women primarily consider so offensive: the quantitative increase of sales distributors and outlets for soft pornography, which makes it a daily discrimination or milieu pollution to visit kiosks, petrol stations etc. Here it is the direct and involuntary confrontation that should be avoided, probably via a display prohibition punishable under the offences chapter of the Criminal Code. To define the sale of magazines with such covers or

contents as a crime according to section 211 of the Criminal
Code would, in my opinion, easily impinge upon other freedom
values, such as the individual's right to privacy, to self-chosen
sexuality, to the most possible free choice of entertainment,
and to freedom of expression—and thus involve the use of
authoritatian paternalism in the attempt to influence the individual's private morality.

Without dignity and with constant violations of integrity, it
is difficult to live a satisfactory life in the eyes of others and
oneself. The concepts 'dignity' and 'integrity' are not ipso facto
connected to material welfare and health, even though access
to such resources—at least when others in one's immediate
surroundings are in possession of them—could promote self-
respect as one of the most central values in human life. On
the other hand, poverty and sickness can increase the risk of
breakdown of an individual's and group's self-respect although
not necessarily so. Others' disparaging view of such stigmata
as need and dependency reinforces the state of and tendency
toward low self-respect. Serious effects can result from an attack
on human dignity and integrity through the breakdown of self-
respect and the production of shame and feelings of guilt for
one's own situation.

Shame and feelings of guilt are hardly an unknown theme in
women studies. Such feelings are usual in victims of rape and
of continual abuse. Not infrequently it appears that shame and
guilt feelings also have effects on one's opinion of one's self
in situations other than those where such infringements have
occurred—i.e., that women's shame can be induced by a far
more 'normal' male controlling force than the openly violent
man. Such mechanisms prompted Høigård and Snare to gather
their women's criminological findings and discussions under the
title 'Women's Guilt' (Høigård and Snare 1983).

Shame and guilt feelings with respect to one's own life and
behaviour patterns, caused by another's infringement and force,
thus represent the most extreme form of the oppression of
women.

Self-Determination and Self-Realization

For John Rawls self-respect is one of the foremost of 'the
primary goods', and this value has two aspects: first of all, a

person's sense of her own worth, her secure conviction that her view of life is right and her plan of life is worth living for; secondly, confidence that one can realize one's plans within the potential of one's own talents and strengths (Rawls 1983:440 f). Rawls thus emphasizes the significance of making a plan of life within the limits of what is possible, and in having confidence that the plan can be realized. The right to self-determination contains, with more or less precision, exactly these elements: the possibility to make independent choices, not only concerning plans of life, but also regarding many everyday duties, and faith in one's own power and talents of realization. The presumption is, however, that the foundation for real possibilities for achieving such autonomy is laid, inter alia, through material justice and legal protection.

The paths and configurations in the life of women are often beset with responsibility for others. Responsibility can be—and often is—self-chosen, but it is also to a large degree forced upon and expected of women, as well as insufficiently valued. Simultaneously, demands are made on women to take part in paid work and politics more or less on a par with men. From a structural perspective this plethora of expectations—housewife expectations coupled with expectations to take part in paid work and expectations of equal status—makes in reality impossible demands. Women can never participate 'on a par with men' in paid work and public affairs, and will never have the same real possibilities as men, since we necessarily must—and gladly— give much of our energy to the work of birth (pregnancy and delivery) and the first child care (breast-feeding and infant care). There are only a few individual women who don't want or cannot have children who can approximate an equal starting point with men. And even then it is most often only a question of 'approximate equality'. The expectations upon mothers and housewives generally associated with women as a group can also have spillover effects on these few individual women in their confrontation with tradition-bound employers and colleagues. The fact that we in addition have the greater part of the post-infant caretaking duties and care of dependents other than children as well, does not bring us any closer to 'equal opportunities' in education and the labour market, which is talked about so much.

Women's periodic interruptions and lesser participation in the marketplace and public affairs are used against them, manifesting themselves in weak employee protection, placement in low wage-earning occupations, weak social security rights, weak employment termination protection, and criticism for lack of political activities. Rather, the necessary and special women functions ought to be included as an integrated and valued part of community life, in such a way that the state becomes 'women-friendly' and that individuals—including men—could make more realistic and natural individual plans of life than today (Hernes 1982:39 f).

Jon Elster defines self-realization as the 'full and free actualizing of the individual's strengths and talents' (Elster 1985:6). As Elster also points out, total self-realization is, however, a utopia. One is forced to choose. Others' needs and wants set moral and economic limits for the individual's self-realization. But the others also create a basis for the same realization. It is always in a certain sense 'with' and 'for' others that self-realization takes place. The duty of society thus becomes the task of organizing the most even possible distribution and breadth of individual and group-prescribed choices. It is the 'freedom to choose' that must be maximized. Even if a person cannot develop all of her talents and needs, she must have as much freedom as possible to choose which of them she will concentrate on. Ex ante, individuals ought to have the utmost possible freedom to choose which sides of themselves they want to realize, because ex post, the roads they did not take will be closed. The formal freedom to choose must of course not be confused with the real possibility of choice. A society cannot guarantee the right to every type of individual fulfilment in life. It will always be a question of distribution of resources and possibilities for general welfare.

Women's law development of birth law and housewives' law is an answer to some of the challenges of self-determination and self-realization, just as money law and paid-work law create the pre-conditions for the development of these values.

If women are to have the possibility to plan their lives at all, self-determined pregnancy and birth are essential rights. Both technology and the law have greatly changed these possibilities after World War II, with the development of and access to means of contraception, and the Termination of Pregnancy Act of 1975 and amendments in 1978 concerning self-determined abortion (Olsnes 1985). Women's interest in determining their own plans of life demands that women should have the means to prevent pregnancy and birth. Moreover, the joy of sex—as far as it is self-determined—also creates a need for accessible contraception and opportunity for abortion. The same devices have admittedly imposed a certain sexual pressure on women, as society's morality and habits have adjusted to the legal and medico-technological changes. But this does not overshadow the essential impact of abortion and contraception, namely that they give women control over their own special sexual property—women's larger sexual potential, as well as their reproduction capability. Self-determination in the administration of this property is of central importance in this context.

Sexuality can be enjoyed. But it can also be sold, and more easily in the case of women that with men. In earlier times one could view marriage as an institutionalized market for the sale of this property. The social and legal system gave women subsistence, first and foremost, through the sexual and reproductive services that she herself or her family sold to a man or to another family. A few such elements continue to be found built into the marriage contract of today.

The objective of birth law is not however primarily to prevent and terminate life in order to lay the foundation for women's self-determined sexuality and time frame for pregnancy. Birth law has also the goal of creating, preserving and developing life. How far the right to create life ought to go is in my opinion one of the most difficult moral questions that now stand on women's political agenda. The technological possibilities that exist today with respect to the manipulation of both motherhood and fatherhood represent powerful ethical challenges. How far ought the law to go in allowing society's assistance in human reproduction? If it goes too far, the pendulum of the value of birth will swing in the direction of considering childlessness an individual sickness, with demands for health service and hospital resources. Even today it happens that childbirth is considered a sickness, and that is regrettable. The rules of maternity allowances have long followed in part the rules of sickness benefits in the National Insurance Act. The education of midwives is to a large extent dominated by the education of nurses, local childbirth homes are being closed down, and childbirth takes place almost exclusively in hospitals etc. (Fastvold 1985 b). But it is a long jump from attaching positive health values to childbirth, to considering childlessness a sickness. We stand at the edge of this leap, impelled forward by medicine's interest in penetrating and mastering the process of creation. But how far does this scientific interest go in coexisting with human values and needs? Will in vitro fertilization (test-tube babies), with manipulation, chosen or deep frozen sperm, or pre-natal diagnosis better human living conditions? What we will permit in the interests of science is one question; how far we go in light of this scientific development towards giving individual rights which can increase one's chances of becoming a mother or father, is a completely different question. How these rights in any case shall be justly distributed raises new problems of a specially moral nature, which still finds itself at an introductory stage of discussion.

Part Two
Three Treatises in Women's Law

6

Women's Right to Money

6.1. Introduction

An independent income of one's own is a prerequisite for participation in and enjoyment of life, privately as well as publicly. Lack of money, on the other hand, gives a person little freedom of movement and a feeling of powerlessness. Consequently, access to one's own money should be considered a minimum welfare requirement in a monetary economy.

This chapter attempts to describe, explain, and evaluate some of the main issues of women's economic position from a legal perspective. By reflecting women's lives and living conditions in legal decisions, the law offers an important source of understanding of women's social situation. However, the effect of legal rules goes beyond this, by contributing to the maintenance and strengthening of women's economic situation. In some instances legal rules can even transform the economic situation of women. Thus the law should not be perceived simply as a passive reflection of economic inequality.

The static nature of legal rules, compared with their dynamic potential, makes research in 'women's law' a fruitful instrument for women's politics. Analyses based on women's law offer a descriptive and explanatory perspective of women's economic hardships, thus indicating paths for women towards greater dignity and influence on society.

Money is allocated between the sexes with considerable injustice in Norway, as in other Western societies. Quite a number of women simply have not attained the minimum welfare requirement: the right to dispose of one's own money. Nor do women in most Western societies receive the money they are entitled to, considering the work they do. This applies not only to work in the home, but equally to traditional wage-earning work in general. Similarly, when sickness and other difficult situations are concerned, women's social needs are not met to the same degree as men's are.

I shall describe some of the legal structures of the economic positions of women in Norway from the point of view of the housewife. Approaching women's right to money from the perspective of housewives is particularly useful because of the fundamental presupposition in the normative structure of the Nordic welfare state that women will marry, and that married women are entirely or partly maintained as housewives, at least for periods of their lives. From a legal perspective, the right of both full-time and part-time housewives to money is weak, and the legal presumption that married women are housewives makes their position even more vulnerable.

This firmly lodged presumption that women are or will be housewives means that money and work are distributed according to specific models for women and men. According to the male model, personal income is provided by way of work outside the home and administered by the linking of the role of breadwinner to that of wage-earner. The female model entails economic dependency and housework, i.e., a privately maintained housewife. The coupling of the role of wage-earner to that of provider has led to a *'provider's rationale'*, administered by men, deeply incorporated into the community of working life and normative system of the welfare state. All this is at the expense of the *'caretaker's rationale'*, administered by women (Hoel, 1981). Both the male and female models of economic provision are secured by a public safety net consisting of social security and the other social benefits of the welfare state. For men these apply in the event of a loss of paid work; for women in the event of the loss of a husband, or the lack of a man where his presence is usually expected (e.g. unmarried mothers).

In Norway as in other countries during the 1970s, women's economic dependency and insecurity were reduced by the increasing number of women arranging their lives on the basis of a mixed model, mostly based on part-time work outside the home. However, this short-term improvement may prove rather hazardous in the long run. When a woman who occupies these two spheres becomes sick, is widowed, or is divorced, she may risk falling between two stools, suffering from being neither a full-time housewife nor a full-time wage-earner—neither a whole woman nor a whole man – and thus not obtaining the full public benefits accruing to either of the two models (Sverdrup, 1981 a).

The connection between economic rights and labour rights for a person wholly or partially enjoying the status of housewife thus makes it necessary to consider money law from the standpoint of housewives. In dealing with this perspective, the primary aim is to present an overall model for money law pertaining to women, in order to throw light on the links between law and society, and between the various sets of rules which effect women. I have chosen to focus on the position of married women, both in the domestic context and in the context of social security. Thus I will not go into the legal postition of unmarried mothers, women in unmarried co-habitation, divorcees, or widows, although these too could be viewed from the standpoint of their position as housewives.

This concentration on married women means that married women's access to money as paid workers will not be treated separately. Nor will taxation be dealt with in depth here, and its significance will only be touched upon in the outline of proposed reforms presented towards the end of the chapter.

6.2. Marriage Contract and Wage Contract

In general, financial obligations are established either by agreement or directly by law. (They may also follow from non-statutory principles). Ordinary debtor-creditor law generally distinguishes between cases where the debtor has assumed an obligation to pay (a contractual obligation), and cases where the obligation has been imposed on him by others, in practice the public authorities (legal obligation) (Kjønstad, 1980).

The two most important types of agreements providing women with their means of economic sustenance are the marriage contract and the wage contract, while the most important legislation is social security legislation. Legal questions particularly pertaining to women are often hard to place in relation to other categories of law. Financial obligations arising through marriage may thus be either contractual obligations or legal obligations depending on which elements of marriage are considered most relevant. The category per se does not necessarily have legal consequences, but the distinction between the two types of financial obligations seems useful when we are discussing the character of the duty of maintenance, because it has consequences for our further work on theory and concepts.

The financial obligations relevant here are those emanating from the mutual duty of maintenance of the spouses codified in Norwegian law and originating at the contracting of marriage (cf. section 1 of the Act on Property Relationship between Spouses of 20 May 1927). Normally the duty of maintenance is a legal obligation, although the question has not been specifically debated (Krüger, 1978; Kjønstad, 1980). This is probably due to the recognition of marriage as a public act, and not a private agreement of the parties, and further to the view that the obligations are directly authorized by law, the specific meaning of which must be determined by an interpretation of the Act.

However, the duty to maintain a spouse differs in several ways from most types of legal obligations, under private as well as public law. The legal foundation of the duty of maintenance has several factors in common with contractual obligations. In my view the specific nature of the duty of maintenance is arguably best evidenced by a comparison with the type of contractual obligation that is most similar to it, namely wages. This comparison will reveal not only the specific nature of the legal obligation of maintenance but also its complex character.

Even though it provides some clues, the Norwegian Act on Property Relationship between Spouses gives few indications as to the contents and the scope of the duty of maintenance, how to comply with it, etc. On the whole, such questions have been left to matrimonial private practice. Thus the legal rules concerning the duty of maintenance are—at least as long as the marriage continues to work—more vague than is usual where legal obligations are concerned. Furthermore, typical legal financial obligations are not aimed at creating a quid pro quo, as is the duty of maintenance. Finally, the contractual basis underlying the duty of maintenance is far more significant than in the case of other legal obligations, which may also be based on agreement to some extent. A comparison between the marriage contract and the wage contract may therefore disclose significant aspects of marriage as a social and legal institution when it comes to the distribution of money and work. Both agreements are entered into voluntarily by two parties on a *formally* equal footing. Both types of agreement are based on reciprocity as regards rights and duties concerning services and counterservices of approximately the same nature. Both types of contract represent *main sources of sustenance* in return for work, the wage contract by providing money in return for work outside the home, the marriage contract by providing maintenance in return for work in the home. Formally, both contracts are gender-neutral; in reality, however, they are both gender-specific.

The marriage contract carries different implications and consequences for men and women. For both the entry into married status is, of course, a rather complex cultural process, with matrimony as the general norm. You may choose whom you marry, and whether or not you should enter into the new status. But for women this process is different from that for men. Their choice on the second matter, especially, is far more restricted. Few women are sufficiently wealthy or independent to consider it worth-while remaining single. Most of us are subjected to social pressure and expectations in this respect from our socialization, from the environment, from work, and from the legal system. Nearly everywhere, full or partial financial dependence is looked upon as the 'most proper' and 'most natural' state for women. Almost every sphere (contractual, social and psychological) is based upon a presumption that private maintenance is and should be a chief source of economic survival for women. Few women enjoy a position in the labour market strong enough to free them to choose an independent life based on their own income from a wage contract.

This comparison with the male wage contract may be carried further. Wage-earners are also free to choose in the sense that within certain limits they may choose to whom they want to sell their work, but not whether they want to sell it. Few women choose to remain unmarried for life, just as men do not choose to remain unemployed, since the large majority of them are not financially independent.

Thus, the marriage contract is gender-neutral in its form, but its effects are gender-specific. The mutual duty of maintenance is expected to be fulfilled by the man bringing in earnings from work outside the home and by the woman receiving private maintenance in return for work in the home, (i.e. 'housekeeping'). One may, of course, also put it like this: the woman contributes towards the maintenance of herself, her husband, and her children by her work in the home. The main point, however, is that the expectation of becoming a housewife is imposed on women at a very early stage, and it assumes the force of law when the marriage contract is concluded (see chapter 7). The woman is expected to take care of the house, her husband, and children; moreover she is often expected to care for needy relatives. The presumption of family care is so strong that, to all intents and purposes, it constitutes a special duty of work for women—although not based on statutory principles because the rules governing marriage are codified in gender-neutral terms. In Norway though, a woman's right to refuse, or to demand equality with her husband, is quite illusory. If he refuses to accept his wife's equal status, she cannot invoke the Equal Status Act, which expressly exempts family life from its area of enforcement (Act on Equal Status between the Sexes of 9 June 1978, section 2, second paragraph).

For women, the marriage contract is considered a primary source of economic survival with the wage contract as a possible supplement. To men, the wage contract (or self-employment) is the main source. For both sexes, however, the subsidiary source of income is social security, the chief legal basis being the *National Insurance Act* of 17 June 1966. This source of income therefore needs to be included in our analysis of the housewife's economic position.

6.3. The Tripartite Maintenance System

Women's economic position may be illustrated by a model of a tripartite system of maintenance (Fig. 1) below, where wages, marriage and social security are placed in a triangular position:

Fig. 1. Sources of maintenance.

Most people move between all three points during various periods of their lives, and some live in all three at the same time. All
the time, however, the main source of income is sex-related, age-
related, and health-related. The triangle reflects the welfare
state's 'female model', thus illustrating the consequences of the
presumption of domesticity as applied to women in Norwegian
law.

During most of their lives the majority of men are subjected
to the wage contract, most of them using their wages to maintain
not only themselves, but their wife and children as well. A close
personal link with the wage contract automatically entails a
close link with social security, because social security represents
a collective insurance against a failure of income, and an accumulated capital to maintain old age's spent labour power.
This means that social security takes over as the economic basis
of survival in the event of unemployment, sickness, accidents,
and old age for that part of the population that has taken part
in wage-earning work. Thus, large parts of the social security
system represent a temporary place of storage for superfluous
or useless labour power, and quite a lot is done to enable insured
people to return to paid work, e.g. through the conditions
governing unemployment benefits, or through special benefits
such as rehabilitation and treatment. Men's strong position in
the labour market therefore means that their position is also
stronger than that of women where social security is concerned.

As I have argued, for many women the marriage contract is
their main source of income, their contribution in the form of
domestic labour being repaid with small and erratic sums of
money for their own use. Where women have taken on paid
work, it is usually assumed to be supplementary to the family's
economy if she is married—because as a rule the man is still
defined as the breadwinner, even if the family economy is dependent on both incomes. However, the fact that all women are
expected to be housewives also affects the position of unmarried
women in the labour market—unless they have learned a trade
or enjoy higher education. So even unmarried women are drawn
towards the system of private maintenance as an economic and
social guarantee of subsistence.

The arrows in the triangle (Fig. 1) are an illustration of these
patterns. The unbroken arrows represent the strongest legal

mechanisms of push and pull in the labour market and social security, whereas the broken arrows are meant to show women's marginal and hazardous position. The broken arrow from marriage to wages indicates that the labour market seldom pulls a married woman from being supported by her husband into a position of self-sustenance through paid work. The unbroken arrow pointing in the opposite direction marks the presumption of economic dependency through which women can be pushed out of the market, partly by low wages and totally by unemployment.

The broken arrow from marriage to social security shows women's situation in the event of divorce from or death of a provider, or when founding a family through childbirth without the presence of a male provider. The unbroken line leading back also illustrates the presumption of dependency, showing how the social security schemes are constructed so that women entitled to benefits lose their rights and are pushed towards private maintenance whenever possible. At the same time efforts are made to push insured women into paid work by various forms of traditional benefits, outside childcare benefits, and educational benefits. In these cases the presumption of dependent housewives is replaced by the expectation that women become paid workers. The rules applying to working women are marked by the unbroken arrow from social security to wages. The broken arrow back illustrates the rights which permanent wage-earning women enjoy if their wages fail or old age liberates them. Thus, a strong connection to the labour market provides social security advantages. High wages result in better benefits; long hours and many years of service give higher return. The benefits thus reflect the wages.

However, wages are a sex-related source of income, quantitively as well as qualitatively, as has been clearly shown in numerous studies of the division of labour between the sexes and women's connection to the labour market. First, there are more men than women in wage-earning work in every age bracket of a working life time. Second, men tend to be more stable wage-earners, staying longer in one job, whereas women go back and forth between marriage and paid work, either simultaneously, or during stages of their life-cycles. Third, men are full-time wage earners, women are usually part-timers. And, of course, men's work is better paid. Women's wages are low, often because their work is a continuation of the kind of work carried out in the domestic sphere. It appears that when nursing, caring or domestic work is industrialized or professionalized, wages are almost invariably low. Moreover, women often get paid less than men for doing the same work, mainly because of the presumption that women have an alternative source of economic support.

Paid work is men's chief source of support, with social security counting as a subsidiary source. Marriage practically never provides a source of maintenance for men.

Marriage is a sex-related source of maintenance, and it is predominantly used by women. However, the number of women maintained by paid work is far in excess of the number of men maintained by marriage. There are in fact, practically no men who are sustained by marriage, and few move between marriage and wages as a source of maintenance.

A married woman's position in social security is consequently weak, at any rate as long as the marriage lasts, and this reflects her economic dependency on her husband. The role of the family breadwinner is connected to paid work, and this connection continues when social security replaces wages as the basis of support. In Norway, nearly 50,000 male old age and disability pensioners receive a maintenance supplement for their wives. Compared with this figure, less than 400 women receive such supplements for their husbands (Annual Report of the National Insurance Administration, 1978). A man therefore benefits from both his own wage-earning work and the work his wife does at home. The maintenance supplements are paid for him, even if she is the one who has laid the foundation for them through her work in the home (the National Insurance Act, section 7-7 old age pension, section 7-8 disability pension, section 4-3 No. 5 unemployment compensation, section 5-5 rehabilitation allowance). The division of work between the sexes at home is matched by a sex-related administration of social security.

6.4. From Appendage to Member

It is probably a question of time how long a Norwegian woman maintained through marriage will continue to be treated so obviously as an appendage to her husband. From a historical point of view, substantial changes have already taken place in this country during the last 10–15 years in this respect. The development of sickness benefits shows this.

Today, housewives are not included in the sickness benefits scheme (the National Insurance Act, section 3-1) nor are they entitled to anything but benefits in kind—hospitalization, medical aid, medicines, etc. (National Insurance Act, Chapter 2). Previously, a housewife was not even entitled to social security in her own right, being a 'subsidiary person' according to the Sickness Benefit Act of 1911. The Sickness Benefit Act of 1956 raised her to the status of 'family member', but not until the enforcement of the National Insurance Act in 1971 did she become an independent member of the Social Security system.

As I have mentioned, housewives do not receive sickness benefits, nor are they entitled to unemployment compensation (the National Insurance Act, section 4-3, No. 2). They are, on the whole, deprived of short-term insurance benefits intended for maintenance. If a woman working in the home should decide to go out to work, and no work is available, she would not be entitled to unemployment compensation regardless of how long she queued up at the labour exchange. Often she is not even registered as unemployed, thus not counting in the employment figures, because only a person who gets unemployment compensation is formally considered unemployed. As the Norwegian Director of Labour has put it, 'Somehow women do not appear as unemployed ... they are maintained somehow' (*Sirene* No. 1. 1974).

Indeed, women's work is considered in a special way in Norway. As a rule, participation in the labour market is a prerequisite for obtaining unemployment compensation—one must have earned wages in order to obtain social security. However, this condition is not absolute. Completed military service (compulsory) is placed on a par with paid work, thus entitling a person to unemployment compensation (the National Insurance Act, section 4-3, No. 4(d)). Work in the home is not valued in the same way, be it ever so useful and necessary (See chapter 8).

The most important social benefit for women is the old age

pension (the National Insurance Act, section 7-1). Old age liberates women financially. Historically, the old age pension developed through much the same pattern as the sickness benefit. Women in Norway obtained the right to an old age pension in 1936, but as a rule the couple's pension was paid to the husband right up to 1971, when women got their own pension paid to themselves.

The Norwegian Housewives' Association has argued that women working in the home should be allowed to work up a pension exceeding the minimum pension amount, that is, they should be allowed to collect supplementary pension points by the state putting a certain value on work in the home. But women past the age of 67 do receive a minimum pension. It seems more important to me to ensure that women receive such minimum benefit before reaching pensionable age than to work for the introduction of a supplementary pension. In any case, it is unlikely that the supplementary pension points would reach a level sufficient to warrant an increase in benefits that is worth mentioning, at least not according to the proposals that have been presented so far (NOU 1979, p. 38). For one thing this money would come too late, and besides, the increase would be too small. The demand for supplementary pension points may have an ideological symbolic function by indirectly raising the value of work in the home, but the question is whether such a symbolic function is worth while.

A disability pension is a long-term insurance benefit that may be granted to housewives (the National Insurance Act, section 8-3), and a considerable number of housewives are receiving such a pension. Originally, under the Acts relating to Rehabilitation and Disability of 1961, it was very hard for housewives to obtain this benefit, regardless of their degree of disability. There has been a gradual change in this respect, yet the amounts payable remain small and limited in a variety of ways (see Bjørnsen, 1979, for a discussion of this).

Research on social security has revealed that female disability pensioners define their situation as disability pensioners differently from males. One reason for this is that a housewife's disability is less discernible, as she is able to carry out as much of her work as the handicap allows. In many ways, housewives who get a disability pension land in the same situation as men who marry: they can carry on with whatever they are doing, and in addition they get something more. Male disability pensioners, however, experience a breach with their earlier existence, which may prove difficult to handle. Joblessness and dependence on a disability pension seem to cause considerable problems for men, who shift from being wage-earners to being pensioners, and frequently define this as a decline in status. Women, on the other hand, seem to consider it an improvement to move from marriage to social security as their source of maintenance (Wærness, 1979).

Women are further discriminated against, depending on their specific status, because the pension may actually differ according to whether the woman is considered to be a housewife or a wage-earner. Childbirth is an even more striking example. Childbirth involves approximately the same effort for all women. Pregnancy, birth, and breastfeeding are obviously a job demanding considerable resources, and ought to result in equal benefits for all. Today, however, housewives receive 20 per cent of the basic amount of the standard social security (as per 1. May 1983 this amounted to NOK 4,520) whereas wage-earning women normally receive a full wage for 18 weeks (the National Insurance Act, section 3-21, Fastvold, 1977). The distribution of the supplementary benefits to handicapped children (the National Insurance Act, section 7-2) is another example. Until recently the administration of these benefits revealed the full effect of the presumption of dependency in Norwegian law, in as much as children of full-time and presumed full-time housewives still have more difficulties in obtaining this benefit than children of potential wage-earning women (see chapter 7).

The substance of the presumption of dependency in Norwegian law is, in short, that all married women are considered housewives until the opposite has been proved. The mother of a handicapped child has to substantiate that she would have been going out to work if she had not had a handicapped child. The benefit is, therefore, not only conditional upon the child's handicap and need of care, but is also based on the fact that the person taking care of the child (in practice the mother) suffers a loss of income. The right to assistance rests with the child: the amount, however, pertains to the situation of another person. The mother has to prove a loss of income in order to qualify for her child's right; and in evaluating her claims the social security authorities have applied an ironclad presumption of domesticity.

Thus, the legal factors tend to be both irrelevant and beside the point when compared to the social and health problems which need to be solved: those who are most in need of support are unlikely to get it, whereas those who already have considerable resources may easily obtain more. The reason is that child care is not defined as the equivalent of paid work, and wages for work in the home are unknown to Norwegian law.

6.5. The Fourth Source

Apart from social security, dependence on a spouse, and regular wage-earning, there is a fourth source of income for women. That is the rapidly growing 'hidden' labour market of nursing, babysitting, and caring for neighbours in need, which is developing as a result of the unreported emoluments that people pay in exchange for services in the local environment. The key point about this labour market is that wages are low and paid on the understanding that they are not registered; if taxes were to be paid together with social security costs, this market would altogether disappear.

A growing number of women in Norway are assumed to participate, mostly on a part-time basis, in the hidden labour market. This has posed problems for both the government and the women involved. To avoid further tax evasions through tacit agreements of this kind, the government has contemplated tax reforms granting a certain level of exemption for this type of work. No proposals have yet been published, however. Obviously, there is a clear although indirect connection between social security benefits, other forms of public support, and this 'hidden' female labour. Quite often insurance money paid to one person in the neighbourhood is used for care by another person. Through these arrangements, the state avoids the costs of a number of caring functions, ranging from nursery schools (of which there is a great shortage in Norway) to institutions for elderly people. The supplementary benefit issued by social security to handicapped children, for instance, is quite often used in this informal way, as are social aid, ordinary benefits to handicapped adults, and other benefits provided by the social security system.

From the women's point of view, tax evasion may to a certain degree compensate for the low wages normally paid in this hidden market. On the other hand, the lack of registration means a total loss of the social benefits women would normally enjoy from ordinary or officially recognized work outside the home. No accumulation of pension points or other rights pertaining to membership in the social security scheme is possible within this system, not to speak of unemployment benefits, which are difficult to obtain even for women in the formal work force. To many women, this is an awkward situation. The typical female work carried out in this hidden market ought to be regulated by statute, including specific tax law provisions, designed to stimulate and channel the valuable work done into forms that are lawful, thus ensuring the workers their right to normal benefits.

As things are today, work in the home is either not valued at all or very little value is attributed to it, even if the work is for other families, and is paid.

I maintain that this situation is an offence to the sense of justice of men and women. I shall elaborate this a little further in order to show the principles involved in the different position of men and women in relation to labour.

6.6. Labour, Money and Justice

Justice, according to the Norwegian legal philospher T. Eckhoff (see chapter 5), may be conceptually split in two, namely equivalent justice and distributive justice. Equivalent justice is aimed at describing situations where values are exchanged between two parties. Money counts as one of the trading objects where both parties presuppose that the objects are connected to each other and are equivalent. Thus, mutuality and equivalence between the parties regarding both rights and duties are central elements of the justice of equivalence.

Money and work are fundamental objects of exchange in this

context. Most labour contracts involve a demand for wages. Within the official job market, a precisely regulated system has been developed through legislation, collective bargaining, agreements, etc. in order to maintain equivalent justice in the individual labour relationship. This is, as I have already mentioned, a system where women for several reasons are severely disadvantaged. The principle of equal pay has not made much of an impact on women's earnings in practice. The main consequence of the sex-divided labour market is that typical women's jobs are low-paid jobs; moreover, in professions dominated by men, women do not attain the same positions as men. Underlying rules and routines regarding the distribution of work and jobs do not create proper conditions for equivalence, not even for women in full-time wage-earning jobs.

Outside the official market, women's pay is even weaker. Important female work carried out in the neighbourhood is often paid mainly, if at all, in kind (food, clothing, a place to live, etc.). Even in marriage, the monetary aspect of equivalent justice is questionable.

The term distributive justice is aimed at situations where a distribution of values takes place on the basis of an entity that exists or has existed. The distribution is taken care of by a distributor allocating benefits (e.g. social security money) or disadvantages (e.g. punishment) to several recipients, and the overall idea is that the recipients shall be placed on an equal footing as far as possible.

Through this type of distribution emerges a series of two-party relationships between the distributor (e.g. a public authority) and the individual recipient (e.g. a member of the social security system). Neither mutuality nor equivalence between the distributor and the individual recipient are at stake in these relationships, but rather the considerations of equality between the recipients.

However, equality is not a uniform concept. Equality in itself may be both unjust and just, depending on which criteria of equality are considered basic and which principles of justice are adopted. One may for instance aim at equality of conditions or of results, according to effort or need, or equality of quantity or quality, etc. The kind of principles of equality and justice which are considered relevant under varying circumstances, is the central analytical and political issue in any assessment of the distribution of money in society.

In my view, the monetary aspect of distributive justice between the sexes and among different groups of women leaves a lot to be desired. Many women have not attained the minimum welfare provision of enjoying the right to the disposal of their own money. Nor do women succeed in having their needs satisfied on a par with men in the case of sickness or in other critical situations. Individual rights to money as a proper foundation for survival and enjoyment of life are far too closely connected to the traditional labour agreement of the market. Thus an unjust distribution of money follows partly from the low valuation of reproduction, and partly from the social distribution of work. Injustices in the market structure are being exacerbated by their effects outside the market structure and beyond private labour relationships. As stated before, the allocation of wages activates a series of public law rights and duties, primarily through the provisions of taxation and social security, and this has considerable impact on the citizens' rights with respect to money.

Public authorities acting as distributors of social security benefits are handling the common property of the citizens. But the principles of equality applied have grown out of the systems of distribution and equivalence in the market, thus being out of tune with the actual overall life and needs of the citizens. Social security is financed through income earned from work, thus wage-earning work is to a large extent taken as the basis for the conditions and stipulations of payment under the National Insurance Act. The principle is equal pay for equal work, instead of social security according to need.

From what has been said above, it would seem appropriate, from the point of view of women's politics, to attempt to strengthen women's position in the market. More important under the present circumstances, however, is the construction of a new justice, created through a gradual dissolution of the twin relationship between social security and wage-earning work: to strengthen the rights of work in the home and to visualize and legalize women's 'hidden' labour without economic losses for the parties involved.

6.7. Reform Proposals

How should we go about ensuring women's greater access to money? It should be justifiable, even in times of recession, to demand that married women be given a direct right to public money, not only a right through men. This means that public allocations in the form of maintenance supplements in social security and tax reliefs, which have their basis in care and maintenance, should go direct to the one who does this work.

In Norway, we have one such direct allocation already, namely the general child allowance, which is a benefit to which the child is entitled, but which is paid to the mother, on the grounds that on the whole it is mothers who take care of the children (Child Benefits Act of 14 October 1946, section 11). In the late 1960s it was suggested that this child benefit should be replaced by a tax deduction for the support of dependent children. However, the proposal was met by such a storm of protests from Norwegian women, who were going to lose control over this money, that the authorities decided to leave the child allowance alone.

In the next round, however, the replacement was in some measure carried out. Tax deductions for the support of dependent children were introduced rather than an increase in child benefit (Act on Maintenance Tax Deduction for Children and Young People of 10 December 1976). Politically, this was less controversial than abolishing the child benefit altogether. The difference between the two schemes—child benefit or tax deduction for the support of dependent children—is evident from who gets the cash. To the family as a whole it makes no difference. The amount is the same. But, whereas the child benefit is paid to the women, the deduction for the support of dependent children is made from the (man's) tax.

Another way of giving women access to money without increasing the child benefit would be to make them into more independent tax subjects. In practice it is possible to maintain the effect of the current child benefit through the tax system. Politically, the one solution may appear preferable to the other. By introducing a tax deduction for the support of dependent children, which is then paid as a negative tax to the person mainly caring for the child but who has no personal income, it would be possible to re-allocate money from men to women. This solution was indicated and suggested, albeit rather vaguely, by the Norwegian Commission of Family Taxation, but has not yet been developed (NOU, 1976, p. 12, Hellum et al. 1979).

There are other ways of re-distribution within the family. The maintenance supplements under social security may, as stated above, be paid direct to women. Tax class 2 (cf. the Taxation Act of 18 August 1911, section 16, first paragraph, and section 75, second paragraph, second sentence) may be replaced by a system of personal deduction and negative tax. Thus, both the tax provisions and the social security provisions may be applied to allocating money to women without extra budgetary expenses.

A more extensive reform would be to transfer cash via the husband's wages. In Norway, this would involve amending the rules of the Act on Property Relationship between Spouses of 1927 with respect to the division of the family income. The issue is a comprehensive and difficult one, and answers can be found only from practical experience. To proceed with this we need more knowledge about how spouses divide their financial resources. In the meantime, I would advocate a reform, the implementation of which should be quite simple, namely to give women working in the home a right to dispose of the common property on a par with that of the husband. At present under Norwegian law she does not get this right until she is divorced or after her husband is dead.

One may also discuss reforms that will involve public expenditure. There are numerous issues to be raised in this connection. As mentioned already, the hidden labour market could be legalized so that participation would not lead to economic loss for any of the parties. This ought to be considered an appropriate reform policy, judging from politicians' recently awakened interest in the potential for human care in the local environment, at a time when placing people in institutions is becoming increasingly expensive.

A more comprehensive approach would be reforms concerning pay for care, housewives' wages, or simply a minimum wage for everybody. Wages paid for caring work may be introduced more or less gradually. An extension of the child benefit may be regarded as a form of wages, and could eventually be formally transformed into a wage. The question of wages for housework is a more complex one, however, not only in practical economic politics, but also within the feminist movement.

The recent international movement for wages for housewives, which developed from roots in Italy and spread to many countries (e.g. Dalla Costa, 1972, Collettivo Internazionale Femminista, 1975), has also had an impact on the Norwegian debate. When all aspects are considered fully, the discussion should—in my opinion—reach beyond the single issue of housewives' wages, and embrace the wider issue of a minimum wage for everybody. This issue is at present the subject of numerous socio-economic studies and reports, and even part of the current reform policies of a number of countries (a survey of the development trends is found in Øyen, 1981). However, when the talk is about 'everybody' getting a minimum wage, one usually has households in mind. But 'everybody' does not usually encompass women or young people. Research projects and reports on this question usually focus on a family model where women and young people are excluded, and a labour market model which leaves out the same groups, because they have not been in the market in a way that gives them the right to be taken into account. The advantage of such a minimum wage based on market and household is sometimes said to be the rationalization of the social security system and social welfare so as to involve less expense for society.

The radical claim, however, would be to discuss a minimum wage on the basis of an individual conception of rights, where 'everybody' above a certain age is a person, and not on the basis of households. This line would bring us closer to the realization of welfare as a minimum income for everybody in our society.

7

Towards a Housewives' Law: The Case of National Insurance for Handicapped Children in Norway

7.1. The Objective of Housewives' Law

There is no housewives' law yet in Norway, but the time has come for its development. Statutes concerning housewives are almost non-existent, but both the situation of being a housewife and the fact that her place of work is her own home give rise to frequent and profound legal consequences. These ought to be defined, systematized, and evaluated.

The marriage contract is the formal basis of housewives' law. The conclusion of the contract creates a relationship between the spouses where both enjoy married status. Statutory rules concerning this married status are, almost without exception, gender-neutral. But in practice the contractual consequences are very different for the husband and the wife. The marriage contract establishes, inter alia, the obligation of spouses to contribute according to their capacity to the maintenance of the family by either providing money or performing activities in the home.[1] However, the responsibility and duty of carrying out work in the home falls almost exclusively on women.

The gender-specific fact that the person who does the housework is nearly always a woman is (1) signalled by the term 'housewife', (2) confirmed by everyday experience, statistical time studies, and sociological studies, and (3) continually nurtured by the expectations of domesticity confronting women from a very early age.

The concepts 'housewife' and 'work in the home' are defined

---

1. The Act on Property Relationship between Spouses of 20 May 1927, No. 1. Section 1.

as follows: a housewife is the person carrying out the necessary functions in her or his own home where the household consists of a nuclear family of two spouses and their children, and the legal questions involved in housewives' law reflect this typical situation. Actually, the housewife's basic task is to work for other members of the household, that is, for her spouse and her own children.

Work at home performed by persons living alone is excluded from the concept 'work in the home'; nor does the concept encompass work performed for persons other than members of the household within the housewife's home, for instance caring for other people's children or industrial or professional work done at home; nor does the concept encompass work for others in other people's homes, such as housemaid's work.

The housewife's duties consist partly of caring for the other members of the household, and partly of household tasks in connection with the running of the home. 'Work in the home' differs from other kinds of work, inter alia, in that it does not provide an income and is not subject to rules on working hours. Thus, the consequences of being a housewife go far beyond one's work in the home and family situation. As indicated above, the civil status of the housewife is basically that of a married person. The marriage contract establishes a status of housewife for women and the legal foundation for the 'housewife rule' in Norwegian law (see p. 149). When a marriage contract is dissolved, the presumption of the housewife rule is usually replaced by a wage-earner presumption, but the strength of the presumption varies according to the basis for the dissolution of the contract. Separation, divorce, and death create transitional situations in which women are given various forms of mixed status as housewives and wage-earners. Such mixed status is also attributed to women living in unmarried cohabitation, unmarried mothers, or women taking care of other family members (parents, etc.) (Gjelsvik & Wankel, 1980).

The working status of the housewife is also variable: (1) She may be a full-time housewife; (2) she may divide her working day between work in the home and paid employment; or (3) she may have full-time work outside and overtime at home. There is a practical legal presumption that married women belong to the first of these three categories, and failing that, to the second, provided they have children or other people in need of supervision in their care. The presumption may be weakened in favour of the third category if the husband has a small income or the woman has a good education or considerable work experience.

Thus, the role of housewife varies, not only from one woman to another and among different groups of women, but also within the lifespan of the individual woman. Proof of this actual or hypothetical role (or what is more likely for the applicant seeking benefits, proof of no such role) gives rise to several legal inconsistencies. The outcome is important because the allocation of the status of 'housewife', or the status of 'wage-earner', or a dual status may be of great consequence for the woman's rights.

The different legal status of housewives and wage-earning women reflects the weak social position of work in the home and the strong social position of paid work. The problem emerges because of the lack of legal regulation of work in the home combined with the housewife presumption that underlies legal assessments of women.

By way of conclusion, one may say that the formal basis of housewives' law is the marriage contract, whereas its actual basis is the life situation of being a housewife. Therefore, this underdeveloped field of law will traverse very varied disciplines, as for instance family law, labour law, birth law, social security law, tax law, and criminal law. Generally, one may say that the *objective* of housewives' law is to study the legal problems particularly affecting women in their status as housewife, future housewife, or former housewife.

Here, I am going to deal with one particular aspect of house-wives' law, i.e. the rule on supplementary benefit to handicapped children. This is a social security rule that provides for an extra benefit for the care of heavily handicapped children. In practice, these children are cared for by their mothers and the benefit is allotted after a close evaluation of the status of the mothers.

By delving into one small sentence in one big complex of law, this chapter intends to provide a cornerstone for a future structure of housewives' law. The provision in question regu-lates the right to supplementary benefit for the supervision and care of handicapped children. It does not say explicitly that the question of benefit concerns housewives or the legal status of work in the home. Such legal invisibility is a characteristic feature of housewives' law. As we shall see later, it is in the hidden assumptions of law that we perceive the housewife.

7.2. The Rule on Supplementary Benefit

Supplementary benefit is a benefit granted to handicapped children and young people below the age of 18. It provides compensation for extra expenditure arising from the special need for supervision and care of handicapped children compared to the needs of healthy children. The main rule is that the benefit will be granted as long as the child resides in his/her own home and that it lapses if the child is placed in an institution. The intention is that the system shall allow the child to be integrated into his/her own environment as an alternative to benefits in kind through institutional care.

By an amendment of 19 March 1971 the rule on supplementary benefit was added as a third sentence to the provision on the ordinary benefit to handicapped people.[2] The wording of the entire rule is as follows:

A person who, after having undergone appropriate treatment, still suffers from a permanent illness, injury, or defect is entitled to an ordinary benefit if he, on account of the illness, injury, or defect, requires special care and nursing or help in the home. The annual ordinary benefit equals 25 per cent of the basic amount. *Where the actual and necessary expenses for special care and nursing of an insured person below the age of 18 are considerably greater, the benefit may be increased [supplemented] in special cases* (my italics).

The ordinary benefit is a long-term benefit aimed at covering definite extraordinary expenses involved in permanent disability. It appears from the wording of the Act that the benefit is granted in two different forms, either as compensation for the supervision and care of the insured person or as compen-

2. The National Insurance Act of 17 June 1966, No. 12, Section 8-2, first paragraph, litra b.

sation for help in the accomplishment of the tasks of the house-hold. The amount of the ordinary benefit is the same for every-body who is entitled to it and amounts to 25 per cent of the so-called basic amount. The basic amount is the index-linked standard amount for all social security calculations according to the National Insurance Act.[3]

The basic requirements for obtaining the ordinary benefit are the same for both adults and children, but the calculation of the amount of benefit is different. The need of a child with respect to supervision and care is assessed without taking into account the care needed by a healthy child of the same age.[4] Only extra care is deemed to involve extra expenditure. Normal care is a private matter inherent in the duties linked to parental authority, and the extent of normal care should be deducted when one is assessing the need for care of disabled children. Thus, disabled children have the benefit of a twofold care sys-tem. Their fundamental needs shall be taken care of by the parents, whereas certain extraordinary needs are provided for by the authorities.

Whereas disabled persons of all ages are entitled to the ordi-nary benefit, the 'supplementary benefit' is a right specifically for disabled children and young people below the age of 18. The right entails a far greater measure of refund of expenses, which, according to the wording of the Act and its legislative history, shall correspond to the actual amount of expenditure.[5] Consequently, this form of benefit may involve comparatively large tax-free cash transfers to the individual family, and it will gradually become a far greater strain on the social security budget than the ordinary benefit. Estimated expenditure on

3. As per 1 May 1980 the annual basic amount was NOK 16,900 (£1336). In Norway today there are about 42,000 people who receive the ordinary benefit, and one in six of these is under 18 years of age.
4. Cf. the Ministry of Social Affairs Regulations of 21 October 1966 on the granting of basic benefits and ordinary benefits, Section 7, second paragraph (abbreviated as the Ministry of Social Affairs Regulations). Following an amendment of the regulations on 17 June 1971 this definition was omitted, although no amendment on the points of fact was involved. See also how the definition has been maintained in the N.I.A. Circular 08-02 of 8 September 1971, updated in 1978, on supplementary benefit (abbreviated in the following the N.I.A. Circular), p. 3.
5. Ot-prp. No. 6 (1970–71) p. 11, Innst. O. No. 25 (1970–71) p. 20, Ministry of Social Affairs Regulations, Sect. 7, paragraph 4.

supplementary benefits in 1980 was £2.7 million (NOK 34.3 million) distributed to 1880 recipients. The expenditure on ordinary benefits to children and young people under the age of 18 was estimated at about £1.7 million (NOK 22.1 million) distributed to 5241 recipients.[6]

What then are the additional conditions for obtaining a supplementary benefit?

As stated above, the insured person must be below the age of 18. Furthermore, the amendment stipulates another four requirements that must be fulfilled: (1) it must be a case of 'actual' expenses; (2) the expenses must be 'necessary'; (3) the expenses must be 'considerably greater' than 25 percent of the basic amount; and (4) the case must be a 'special' one.

The maximum age rule is easy to apply because it is objective. But the reasoning behind it is rather obscure. It was stated in the legislative history that the 18-years age limit 'is related to the fact that from this age disabled children are entitled to a disability pension'.[7] The legislature plainly regarded the supplementary benefit as compensation for not being entitled to a disability pension, thus constituing assistance for general living expenses. At the time the provision on supplementary benefit was passed and came into force in 1971, the minimum age for being entitled to a disability pension was 18 years, which was in accordance with the ordinary age transition from being maintained to becoming self-maintained. However, following an amendment in 1975, the minimum age for receiving a disability pension was reduced to 16 years, whereas the upper age limit for being entitled to a supplementary benefit was not reduced correspondingly. The lack of harmonization in 1975 emphasizes the obscurity as to what the benefit is supposed to cover.

Whereas a disability pension is a benefit designed to cover the general cost of living, that is, a maintenance aid, and the ordinary benefit to children is supposed to cover extra expenditure incurred by disability, and is therefore a benefit designed to cover the cost of care, the supplementary benefit is a rather vague combination of both.

Guidelines for the interpretation of other parts of the legal

6. The source of the computations is Table No. 2 of program package SE08 A 104, N.I.A. Statistics, as per 31 December 1979.
7. Ot-prp. No. 6 (1970–71), comments on Section 8-2, p. 15.

text are few and far between. One might expect to find clearer statements as to the meaning of the terms 'actual', 'necessary', 'considerably greater' and 'special case' in the legislative history. Such statements are unclear or non-existent. As for the purpose of the Act, however, the legislative history is unambiguous. The legislators wanted to provide families with handicapped children with adequate economic support 'to enable them to keep the child at home', both because integration was generally believed to give a better prognosis for the handicapped person, and because it was going to be less expensive for society.[8]

The legislative intent was that home care was to be preferred to institutionalization. In the light of this policy the guidelines for discretion as to which cases are 'special cases' are such that basically, to be 'special' the child must be so heavily disabled that it needs to be placed in an institution. It would then be up to the social security authorities to assess the child's need for care and compare this with the family's capacities and possibilities of taking over society's responsibility in return for a compensation for the extra expenditure involved. Section 7, paragraph 2, of the Ministry of Social Affairs Regulations states that the benefit may be supplemented 'provided this gives the insured person a greater possibility to continue living in his own home'. But 'the fact that it would not have been natural, appropriate or possible to place the child in an institution if the relatives had found it difficult to keep the child at home' is in practice no argument for refusal (cf. the National Insurance Administration Circular, p. 3). Nor is the fact that the child has been institutionalized any reason for refusal. The Social Security Tribunal decision in appeal case No. 2318/74 stated that 'the court considers it to be of considerable importance that the appellant maintain contact with the family and may spend his school holidays at home', and awarded a supplementary benefit in order to cover holiday expenses.

It is not clear from the legislative history what kind of extra expenses are acceptable to the authorities or how they are to

8. Ibid. pp. 1,9,11,15, Innst. O. No. 25 (1970–71) p. 20. See also the general attitude in St.meld. No. 88 (1966–67) Om utviklingen av omsorgen for de funksjonshemmede (Report to the Storting on the Development of the Welfare System for Disabled Persons) and Innst. S. No. 263 (1967–68), which formed part of the basis for the amendments in 1971.

be computed. All we are told is that in principle there is no upper limit to the benefit.

So, what we have here is a pattern of legal sources displaying well-known features of the Scandinavian welfare state: the statutory provision is brief with wide powers, and the legislative history provides few guidelines or none at all for the subjects which are left to discretionary consideration according to the Act (Kjønstad, 1978). The regulations issued by the Ministry of Social Affairs contain some detailed definitions—to which I shall revert later—but these too are scanty. It is in the agencies and bodies involved in the administration of social security that the rule-making takes place, with the National Insurance Administration as the highest rule-making authority in practice and the Social Security Tribunal as the highest administrative authority. The legislative branch has been content with the role of maker of the statutory framework.

7.3. The Cases and the Clients

The decisions of the Social Security Tribunal (S.S.T.) provide the most relevant and authoritative insight into current law and practice. The documents also enable one to look into the practices of the National Insurance Administration (N.I.A.). I have therefore studied all the cases appealed to the Tribunal concerning supplementary benefit between 1 July 1971, when the Act came into force, and 1 July 1978—a total of 83 cases during the first seven years of the Act. Of these, 70 cases were decided, and 13 were dismissed by the Tribunal after changes were made by the N.I.A. during the appellate proceedings before the Tribunal, changes that mostly favoured the appellant.

The documents make dramatic and pathetic reading. They call forth pictures of helpless children in utmost need and of parents who are striving for a life together with them. These children often need continuous supervision and round-the-clock nursing: they must be helped to the toilet or they may need nappies until far into their teens; bedding and nappies may have to be changed several times a day; they may have to be carried upstairs and downstairs on someone's back; they must be helped to and from their wheelchairs and into the taxi that takes them to the special nursery; they may be physically passive children, even needing someone to scratch their backs, or they may be hyperactive or self-destructive children, a danger to their surroundings if they are not watched. 'Nobody who does not live like this can imagine what it is like', says one appellant. 'In a way the whole family is handicapped', writes another. Parents—and especially mothers—are wearing themselves out physically and mentally; their backs hurt and there are other signs of injuries due to the constant care as the years pass and the children get heavier and more difficult to carry. There are married people who have not had one single night to themselves since the child was born. Brothers and sisters do not get sufficient attention. And so the sad true tales go on.

It is the interpretation of the terms 'actual' and 'necessary' expenses that dominates the cases, both of which are requirements for granting the benefit and at the same time yardsticks for measuring the extent of the benefit.

It is not sufficient to demonstrate an actual and essential need for care, a need of such a character that it would usually involve substantial expenditure. In Section 7, paragraph 4, the regulations of the Ministry of Social Affairs require that the actual expenses must be documented or loss of income shown to be probable, and the N.I.A. is very strict in its interpretation of the demand for documentation. However, in several cases the S.S.T. changed the practice of the N.I.A. by making less strict demands as to the proof of expenses incurred where the need for care was exceptionally great.

According to Section 7, paragraph 1 and also paragraph 4, of the regulations, the expenses may be divided into two categories: either expenses for 'paid home help' or 'aid from members of the family'. Home help expenses can be covered either in the form of care of the child—that is a direct care benefit—or as a household benefit for relief in the ordinary housework, for instance so as to give the mother more time to take care of the child. Paid home help was intended as the primary scheme according to the regulations, and yet the cases concerning paid help are few. It seems that those who cannot afford a housemaid do not claim supplementary benefits. This is because it is the practice of lower decision-making bodies to require an already existing arrangement for paid home help before supplementary benefits are paid. Those who can afford it may hire a maid and hope for a favourable outcome of the claim for benefit. The less well-off are unable to arrange for help, and some do not hire help because it is difficult to find someone, or they may want to do the caring themselves.

Appeal case No. 1598/74 is an example of a family that did not have the means to hire help. The N.I.A. accepted that there was a need, but rejected the claim because no prior arrangement had been made for help. The S.S.T. reversed the decision on the grounds that the mother's likely loss of income (due to the handicapped child) was greater than 50 per cent of the basic amount.[9] In case No. 1037/74 (2497/74), the County Board and the N.I.A. decided to grant the benefit 'from the date when help was available'. The S.S.T. judged that the benefit must be granted even if no arrangement for help had been made, and that it should be up to the parents of the appellant to choose whether they would hire help or undertake the care themselves.[10]

In case No. 2505/73 the N.I.A. in my opinion displayed a somewhat unrealistic idea of what kinds of families have permanently employed home help today. The claim for refund of expenses for home help was rejected with reference to the fact that it was necessary in any event for parents who were working outside the home and who had minor children—9 and 11 years old—to have a housemaid. The S.S.T. did not agree; nor did the S.S.T. agree with the N.I.A. in a similar case No. 6/74. The S.S.T. stated: 'Where the children are so old (17 and 15 years) a parent or parents who are working outside the home are not always likely to have a housemaid—it would depend on the circumstances'.

Practice has led to a shifting of the focus in applying the law away from paid home help, such as was initially intended, to focusing on family members as the central providers of care.

Some support for this practice is to be found in the legislative history—that is, if one goes a little beyond the direct statements on supplementary benefit and looks to the intentions behind the integration measures for handicapped children set down

9. See also cases Nos 889/74, 913/74, 1418/74, 1339/76.
10. See also cases Nos 1339/76 and 910/74 on parents' freedom of choice. In No. 504/74 the S.S.T. seems to base its decision on a stricter evaluation of the demand for documentation. No. 743/73 was also affirmed.
11. See case Nos. 2101/74 and 2505/73.

throughout the same legislative document. Both in the prelimi-
nary Report to the Storting and in the Government Bill there
were several statements concerning:

> ... the desirability of employing to a larger extent the work-
> force represented by the mothers of these children.... Con-
> sidering the far too small number of institutions, it might be
> a good investment to help to enable the mothers to provide
> *heavily handicapped children* with appropriate care and up-
> bringing (my italics).[12]

Reference was also made to the considerable lack of expert staff
and to the fact that better exploitation of the mothers' working
capacity would enable the specialists to concentrate their work
with the child on what was necessary:

> ... since the mother, who ordinarily will also have a *strong
> motivation,* can give the child the necessary individualized,
> *round-the-clock* care (my italics).[13]

The legislature's expectations where mothers are concerned
seem very much to have been fulfilled if we look at the reality
behind the cases on supplementary benefit. It really is the
mothers themselves who take care of their children. Thus, the
practical effect of the Act is that certain requirements for granting the benefit are connected to the characteristics of one person, i.e. the child. Other requirements for granting the benefit,
and the computation regulations, are connected to the characteristics of another person, i.e. the child's mother. A number of
problems are inherent in this specific type of coupling of people
within one and the same legal rule.

7.4. Discrimination between Mothers

As for help from members of the family, the regulations require
that this 'must be so comprehensive ... that their wage-earning
potential is considerably reduced' (Section 7, paragraph 1).

12. St. meld. No. 88 (1966–67) p. 53 and cited in Ot. prp. No. 6 (1970–71) p.
12.
13. St. meld. No. 88 (1966–67) p. 20.

The requirement that actual expenses be proved means in this connection that the member of the family who undertakes the nursing must document or substantiate the likelihood of *a loss of income.*

The loss of income presupposes wage-earning work. If the mother is the one who stays at home to take care of the child, the rule is that the expenses involved in caring for the child will be refunded if the mother would have been engaged in wage-earning work if the child were a healthy one. No extra expenses are deemed to be incurred if the mother would have stayed at home in any case. In practice, therefore, disabled children who are being taken care of by mothers regarded as housewives will not be covered by the supplementary benefit scheme. The peculiar fact facing us here is that the legal status of the housewife is very weak, while the potential wage-earner's work in the home generally is of far greater value than usual. A woman who could have engaged in wage-earning work, but who chooses to stay at home, will find that her work of care results in compensation for lost income because she is considered a potential wage-earner, whereas she who would have been a housewife gets nothing—for doing the same work!

Naturally, these different legal consequences of the socially beneficial work of mothers give rise to a number of dubious situations.

Because the legal consequences connected with the status of housewife and the status of potential wage-earner are so widely different, the question of status becomes the central issue in the cases in which it is the mothers who take care of their children. And these are the majority of cases, more than 90 per cent.[14] Therefore, their rights depend (1) on whether they are given the status of housewife or whether they succeed in being regarded as potential wage-earners, and if they succeed, (2) on the extent of their wage-earning and what kind of work they would have engaged in. The central issue in all these cases is whether the

14. In several cases the question has been raised whether fathers have sustained loss of income by having had to stay at home more than fathers usually do, so that they have had to find work at the place where they live, or could not work overtime. See Nos 1806/73, 2318/74, 3355/74, 1856/75. In case No. 1518/74 the mother was ill and the father's loss of income was the main issue. In case No. 910/74, the chief issue was also the father's loss of income.

mother can substantiate a claim that she would have been earning an income if it were not for the disabled child, and also the amount of the loss of income according to probable working hours and type of work.

In order to be taken into consideration at all, the loss of income must be of a certain size. According to the wording of the Act it must be 'considerably greater' than 25 per cent of the basic amount, which equals the ordinary benefit. In Section 7, paragraph 2, of the regulations, this is interpreted so that the expenses must amount to at least twice that, i.e. 50 per cent of the basic amount. In practice, this lower limit often proves to be a source of difficulty.

7.5. What Counts as Evidence in Housewife Cases?

The starting point is the alleged loss of income. The question whether there is a loss of income is decided in the light of a number of factors on the basis of discretion. However, the information treated as evidence generally falls into three categories, so that one may actually talk of applied directives for the exercise of discretion. It will be a question of (1) the mother's possibilities of obtaining paid work at the place where the family lives; (2) the mother's previous education and occupational experience; and (3) the mother's actual caring responsibilities for people other than the disabled child.

These are the systematically used and most relevant factors. Additional factors are the mother's motivation for taking paid employment, whether she has shown/shows a willingness to go out to work, what it would cost to work compared to staying at home, and the total economic situation of the family, especially viewed in the light of the husband's income.

A study of the cases shows that the practice of the N.I.A. and the S.S.T. reveals distinctly different patterns of weighting and balancing these factors. The Tribunal, to a far greater extent than the N.I.A., accepts the mother's assertion that she would in all probability have been working had it not been for the disabled child. This also means that, in a number of cases, the Tribunal calculates the expenses differently from the N.I.A. by coming closer to the mother's estimates as to (1) the nature and amount of work outside the home, and (2) deduction for expenses.

On all points the N.I.A. may be said to argue more in favour of the housewife solution. The decisions of the Tribunal represent a counterweight; they show that the Tribunal does not attach so much significance to the factors considered by the N.I.A., to indicate 'domesticity'. Instead the Tribunal emphasizes the likelihood of wage-earning status. However, there is harmony between the two with respect to the types of factors found to be of importance; the discrepancy is in the weighting of the factors involved.

From the outset the labour market situation in the child's home district has been an important factor in the application of the law. Case Nos 1693/73 and 2897/74, both confirmed by the S.S.T., were cases in which the limited opportunity for work where the mother lived was a significant factor. In two other cases (Nos 1106/74 and 1017/77) the opportunity for work was considered to be small, but the S.S.T. still reversed the N.I.A. decision. In one case (No. 889/74) the N.I.A. and S.S.T. evaluated in different ways the availability of work for unskilled labour in the district, and in another case (No. 2959/74) the S.S.T. criticized the N.I.A. for requiring that the mother be able to present proof of concrete plans for employment.[15]

The N.I.A. has often refused claims for supplementary benefit by attaching decisive importance to this factor of work availability. If there were jobs available in the neighbourhood, it was possible for the woman staying at home to obtain aid. Where there were no jobs available, for instance in thinly populated areas, a woman staying at home received no aid; though her child required the same care. Market studies were undertaken, statements from employment agency authorities were collected, and the mother was practically required to present concrete plans for work outside the home, as well as job offers.

The S.S.T., however, assessed these cases differently, focusing less on the objective labour market situation and the subjectively alleged plans for work. To some degree the labour market factor has gradually been replaced by the Tribunal focusing more on the individual characteristics of the mother of the handicapped child.

15. See also Nos 2345/73 and 3329/74.

One factor often taken into account is the mother's education and previous work experience, and quite naturally so, since it is her status as a potential wage-earner which is to be assessed. In 28 per cent of the cases this was a point of major interest in the N.I.A.'s assessments, and in some of the cases the central focus. The cases fall into two groups: one group—nine cases —concerned various kinds of educational background and work experience; the other group—farm-women—raised particular problems in seven cases. Every year since the supplementary benefit began, the general tendency of the N.I.A. has been to assess the qualifications and experience of the mothers of handicapped children lower than the Tribunal.

The mothers whose education the N.I.A. did not consider to be adequate for a potential wage-earner status, included two nurses, one hospital laboratory technician, one telegraph assistant, three women who had gone through commercial college and who had office work experience, one owning a shop, and one with a university education. Many of them had considerable work experience before their disabled child was born, and some of them had been working part time after the child was born. The Tribunal took a more positive view of the educational and work experience necessary for the status of potential wage-earner and tended to decide that it was likely that the woman would have been employed if she had not had a handicapped child, or that she would have been more extensively employed. In seven of the first group of nine cases the Tribunal's decision was made in 1977.[16] In 1975 the Tribunal had reversed an N.I.A. decision, referring to reports by the Equal Status Commission and to studies of the labour market showing an increased tendency of employment among married women with children.

A clear example of the position taken by the Tribunal is illustrated by the only case involving a woman with a university education. She was working part time but said that she would have been working full time outside the home had it not been for the child. She maintained that she had obtained higher education with the intention of making full use of it, and that she had engaged trainees and other help to take care of the

16. Nos 719/74 and 431/75 (nurses), 2950/74 (hospital laboratory technician), 542/75 (telegraph clerk), 1598/74, 1017/77, 1587/75 and 2319/74 (shop assistants and office workers), 1736/74 (owner of a shop), 431/75 (academic).

healthy children—she did not claim a refund for these expenses. She did, on the other hand, demand compensation for the loss of a half-time job, because she wanted to stay at home with the disabled child when the child was not in a special day nursery. The N.I.A. refused; the Tribunal accepted the claim.

In all the cases involving farm-women there was a tendency on the part of the N.I.A. to give their work on the farm a low status, allegedly because a lot of their time is used for housework regardless of whether they have disabled children or not. Such a legal assessment of farm-women's work on the farm is not unusual in other administrative bodies either (Rognlien, 1977). However, here too the decisions of the Tribunal were much more likely to be in agreement with the claim of the applicant.

The S.S.T. reversed five of the seven cases involving farm-women.[17] In one case (No. 2423/73) the S.S.T., judging from the record, was stricter than usual in its evaluation. In another case (No. 743/73) the N.I.A. decision was also confirmed. Five of the cases concerning farm-women were settled by the S.S.T. in 1977. In one other case (No. 910/74) the mother having the care of the child was also a farmer, but here it was the father's loss of income that was at issue, as he had to stay at home from shrimp-fishing to help the mother with the care of the child and with the farm work.

Several of the disabled children in question were taken to a day nursery or a special school—usually a day nursery for handicapped children—for some hours every day. This was the situation in 27 of the cases, and the N.I.A. considered this important in two different ways. Partly, it was said that the mother's wish to go to work was not strong enough if she did not use the hours when the child was away at the nursery to go to work; and partly, it was said that the need for care was not great enough if she actually had a few hours off every day.

Both types of argument were on the whole overruled by the S.S.T. In the opinion of the Tribunal it was not reasonable to expect the mother of a severely disabled child to have the time and the strength to use the hours when the child was away to go to work, as this was the only time she had to get through the rest of the housework. Her not working could thus not be

17. Nos 1753/73, 1037/74, 2497/74, 1438/74, 1917/76, 1727/75.

taken to imply that she would not have been working if the child had been healthy. Furthermore, even though the child was admitted to a day nursery, the need for care could still be great enough to be deemed 'necessary'.

Tribunal reversals were generally based on different factors, where the day nursery factor and the question of sisters and brothers often crossed each other. In four cases (Nos 6/74, 2815/74, 118/74 and 1372/74) the S.S.T. stated that it was unreasonable to demand or to expect the mother to engage in work outside the home while the handicapped child was at school or at the day nursery.

When the child requires extensive care, the mother needs these hours to do the housework. Even if there are other persons needing to be cared for by the mother while the handicapped child is at the day nursery, the claim for supplementary benefit may be granted. In No. 1372/74 the S.S.T. stated 'even if the parents have two younger children, the court has found that in this case the care of the appellant must be so burdensome that it must be considered a real obstacle to seeking employment outside the home'. In No. 1106/74 the mother also had to take care of a mentally retarded sister and an old mother. In quite a number of cases of this type the N.I.A. decision was reversed by the S.S.T. There are very few cases of this type where the S.S.T. confirmed the N.I.A.; some stand out from the rest (see, for example, NOS 2340/73 and 665/75). In cases where the S.S.T. confirmed the decisions of the N.I.A., the information is usually scanty, which makes them harder to assess.[18]

As previously stated, the Tribunal has focused on 'the need for care' to such a degree that the demand for proof of status as a potential wage-earner and documentation of expenses has been relaxed in some cases. It was stated that the 'need for care' could be so overwhelming as to be a complete and absolute barrier to working outside the home.

In several cases in which the Tribunal relaxed the demand for documentation of expenses, the Tribunal also stated that it was up to the parents themselves to choose whether to engage help or sustain a loss of income because of the disabled child.[19]

18. For typical examples of this, see Nos 1106/74, 507/76, 1917/76, 431/75, 3355/74.
19. See Nos 1037/74, 2497/74, 1339/76, 910/74.

According to N.I.A. practice, the factor that weighs most in deciding to grant housewife status is that the mother is caring for other minor children. The frequent reference to it and the weight attached to this factor have played a considerable role in N.I.A. decisions. There were 34 such cases in which other children were considered a greater obstacle to the mother's engaging in work than her care of the disabled child. On this point the N.I.A. went far in assessing the need for care of healthy children. In many cases this need was said to last until the child had been in school for some years, in one case until the ages of 18 and 14, in another 11 and 14 and in several others over 10.

It also happened that the care of perfectly healthy husbands, was considered to be an obstacle to the mother's engaging in work.

On the other hand, it was not considered a decisive argument for the granting of wage-earning status that arrangements were made for help with the other healthy children, or that there were clear offers to look after them.[20]

The N.I.A. also considered responsibility for one's own mother and mother-in-law or a mentally handicapped sister a weighty obstacle to the mother of the disabled child engaging in work. In case No. 1162/74 the fact that the mother took on the care of other people because the disabled child kept her at home in any case apparently did not receive sufficient attention as a counter-argument.

The N.I.A.'s strigent assessment of the amount of care and supervision required by healthy children not only raises illusory obstacles to the mother engaging in work, it also reduces the N.I.A.'s assessment of the amount (and valuation) of 'extra care' required by the handicapped child. In one case (No. 2128/73) it was declared a general rule that disabled children under two years old could not receive supplementary benefit because every child below the age of two needs much care and attention.

20. Nos 1037/74 (2497/74) (18 and 14 years old, the handicapped person 20, mother owning a shop), 431/75 (spouse as well), 463/75 (grandmother looking after healthy children), 1098/75 (three children above 10 years of age), 2345/73 (two children of school age, mother single provider). See also Nos 1524/73, 1916/74. All the cases mentioned, save No. 463/75, were reversed, Nos 463/75, 503/74 and 3116/74 (brothers and sisters of school age) were confirmed.

The S.S.T. stated that such grounds for refusal were not recognized by law—and so the N.I.A. followed up by updating the departmental circular, which now underlines that the two-year limit is a general rule only. In another case the N.I.A. refused to accept expenses incurred in engaging a babysitter for a disabled child of 11 years as extra expenditure, as such expenses were said to be normal. The parents in this case maintained that when their oldest and healthy daughter was 11 years old, *she* was the one who was babysitting. The Tribunal agreed with the parents (No. 542/75).

In one case the S.S.T. subjected the age issue to a more fundamental assessment and confirmed an age limit of three years as a kind of lower limit for when it was considered natural for a mother to seek outside employment. The age limit was linked to public statistics on the trend of the frequency of married women engaging in wage-earning occupations. Such a three-year limit also conformed more with practice in other connections. In its departmental circular the N.I.A. introduced a requirement that the disabled child's siblings be over 3 years of age for the mother to attain a status of wage-earner, unless otherwise warranted by special considerations.

7.6. The Housewife Rule: A Summary of the Findings

Looking at the cases we find that a 'housewife rule' underlies cases involving married women who have disabled children in their care, a rule strictly applied by the N.I.A., less strictly by the S.S.T.

In fact there seems to be a general 'housewife rule' applied to women in Norwegian law, both as a rule determining status and as a rebuttable presumptive rule of evidence similar to the *pater est* rule for men. The marriage contract has several legal consequences, one of which is that married women are given the status of housewife. The housewife rule differs from the *pater est* rule in that the criteria for housewife status are vague and vary within the same field of law as well as from one field of law to another.

As both a rule of status and a rule of evidence, the housewife rule stems from marriage and may be formulated as follows: a married woman has the status of housewife until the opposite is legally proved through the attainment of rights as a wage-earner or potential wage-earner. The status of housewife has legal consequences which in most cases are characterized by the lack of benefits attached to this status. The housewife does not accumulate pension points in the general social security scheme and is therefore not entitled to supplementary benefits, sickness benefit, or unemployment compensation; her rights in connection with childbirth are very weak, she is not insured against work-related injuries, the criteria for allowing her separate tax assessment are very strict, her claim for disability pension is often rejected and, if she gets it, the amount is sure to be small. Besides—as I have shown—disabled children of housewives are in practice not covered by the supplementary benefit, unless an arrangement is made for hiring home help. The housewife exists as the husband's economic appendage, entailing a dependent supplement for support of a dependent under Social Security and a deduction for support of a dependent on his income tax.

The housewife rule becomes important as a rebuttable presumptive rule of evidence, both inside and outside family law, in cases in which the status of full-time or part-time wage-earner is alleged. A woman may claim her rights on a factual basis: that wage-earning work actually has been carried out, for example, the claim for separate tax assessment of farm-women. Or the allegation may be made on a hypothetical basis: that the applicant would have had the status of wage-earner, had she not been handicapped herself or if she had not had a handicapped child.[21] The aim of the allegation is to obtain the benefits resulting from having the status of wage-earner compared to the status of housewife.

The housewife rule appears to be applied as a rather strict rule of evidence. There are stringent requirements for proving that a status of wage-earner exists or would have existed, and the burden of proof rests on the woman.

Where unmarried and divorced women are concerned, the housewife rule as a rule determining status no longer applies. They are, on the contrary, regarded as self-supporting or supporters of children almost on a level with men.

21. The evaluation of the status of disabled women often gives rise to difficulties, see N.I.A. Circular 08-02 on the right of housewives to disability pension and to ordinary benefit for help in the home, of 19 September 1970.

For single parents the situation is normally the opposite to that of married women: a presumption of wage-earning results in loss of public benefit. The strength of the presumption varies with the ages and number of children. Yet it happens that the housewife rule as a rebuttable presumptive rule of evidence can even have an effect on the situation of single parents. In five of the cases on supplementary benefit the N.I.A. designated single parents as having either a full or partial status of housewife. The Tribunal changed the presumed status in three of the cases —in one of them with specific reference to the fact that the mother was a single parent and that it therefore must be considered likely that she would have been going out to work, even if it would have involved carrying a considerable burden.[22]

7.7. Conclusion: Implications of the Application of the Housewife Rule in Cases of Handicapped Children

In general, the justification for the housewife rule is questionable, but in cases of supplementary benefit, there can be no doubt that the application of the rule leads to injustice and inequality.

The inequality is manifested in the differences between the National Insurance Administration and the Social Security Tribunal with respect to their decision-making processes. They quite often arrive at different results by attaching varying weight to the same factors of significance. It is argued that the feedback from the decisions of the Tribunal in the form of altered guidelines within the N.I.A. contributes in the long run to the harmonization and establishment of applicable law.

However, in these cases I do not believe that such a model for the development of the rule of law would be workable in and of itself. The subject matter is too scattered, the factors to be evaluated too numerous, and the discretions involved are open to being separated, linked to each other, or aggregated as one wishes. Therefore, the field is open to a general application of values and ideology at the expense of rules of equality.

22. No. 2345/73 referred to a presumption of wage-earning work for a single provider. Case Nos 913/74 and 468/78 were reversed, whereas No. 545/75 was confirmed, with reference to, inter alia, the separated father being able to take care of the disabled child.

The evidence shows that this is the case even within the S.S.T. There are considerable differences among the various judges. Interesting professional differences also emerge, in that the judges who are experts on medical treatment and rehabilitation tend to agree with the N.I.A. in its harsher criteria, more often than do the professional legal judges.

The injustice follows from the housewife rule itself. As a result of the coupling of the mother and the child, the child's need for care has been neglected as a subject for consideration. Furthermore, the emphasis on the mother has nothing to do with the nature and extent of her nursing and special care for the child, but rather is concerned with her hypothetical opportunities and duties in entirely different connections.

(a) If the mother has only gone through primary school and has little work experience, the child's rights will be rather weak. And if supplementary benefit is granted, the benefit will be small even if the need for care is considerable. If, on the other hand, the father's income is also small, the chances of a supplementary benefit are improved because the presumption of the mother's housewife status will then be weakened.

(b) If, on the other hand, the mother enjoys a good education and extensive work experience, the benefit to the child will be larger, even if the need for care is not so great.

(c) If the child lives in a place with few employment opportunities for women, the right to supplementary benefit will be weak. This will also be so if the claim for the benefit is filed at a time when market trends show a low demand for female labour.

(d) If the disabled child has brothers and sisters whom the mother also cares for, the disabled child's rights will be reduced. The same occurs if the mother has other people to take care of, for instance an old grandmother, a sick aunt, etc. The heavier the mother's burden, the weaker the rights of the disabled child.

It is easy to understand why both the families in question and the social service workers have difficulties in accepting these inherent inequities and injustices. Several cases reveal that the parents simply do not understand why they do not get the benefit. Moreover, three different studies of the practice at three local social security boards show that the welfare officers react negatively to the rules. They point to the large percentage of rejections of claims for supplementary benefit, and they believe the rejections to be arbitrary and to have unreasonable consequences. Some researchers have exerted pressure in order to bring about a change in the rules (Wahl & Bohne, 1973; Saetness, 1977; Kolberg & Benum, 1979).

Obviously, it is both reasonable and correct that families with severely handicapped children should get sufficient assistance to enable them to keep the child at home instead of at an institution. Possibly, they should also receive a special maintenance benefit, but here is not the place to discuss this.

It is equally obvious that such assistance should be given for hired help as well as to a mother who has the care of the child. In that case the issue to be evaluated must be in conformity with the kind and extent of the care, irrespective of who does the work and regardless of whether the mother would like to or would be able to engage in wage-earning work outside the home.

Under the present circumstances, the housewife rule results in the irony that the more qualified the mother is for carrying out the work in the home, the smaller the chances of the family getting assistance. If there ever was an example of society's exploitation of the housewife, this must be it.

Postscript

Since this chapter was written the rules on supplementary benefit for handicapped children were altered by the Act of 30 June 1981. Regulations are now more detailed than before, and more weight is put on the child's need for care when the benefit is assessed. The right for the child to obtain the benefit, however, still rests on the mother's loss of income, as before. Whether these changes have brought about any relief in the pressure on these heavily burdened families, can only be assessed through a wholly new investigation into the practice of the law.

8

Discrimination between the Unemployed

8.1. Introduction. The Problem

Article 110 of the Norwegian Constitution imposes a duty upon the State to create the conditions which make it possible for every person who is able to work to earn a living by work. This principle is followed up to a lesser degree for women than for men. For many women this right to paid work is never realized even though they want to work, and woman's work in the home gives no means of support in the form of one's own income.

Not even with respect to society's next-best solution—subsistence cash payments when suitable work cannot be found—do women have rights equal to men's. Women outside the official work force are denied the right to unemployment compensation when unemployed, even if they officially report to the Employment Office as persons seeking employment. Furthermore, women who perform both care work in the home and paid work outside the home are often in a weaker position than men with respect to the labour market. As a result women more often than men are both excluded from the marketplace and ineligible for social security benefits.

The aim of this chapter is to give an account of women's position on the basis of the rules for unemployment compensation and to evaluate the rules with respect to the various unemployment situations in which women find themselves.

Authority and Administrative Procedure

Unemployment compensation is the oldest and most important of all the various kinds of social security benefits or payments for the unemployed, authorized in the National Insurance Act (N.I.A.) of 17 June 1966, No. 12, section 4-1 (a). The objective is to provide temporary financial support through partial compensation for the loss of income due to unemployment (N.I.A. sections 1-1, 4-3). Other social security unemployment benefits have grown significantly within the last decade, but they will not be dealt with here (the various benefits and payments are listed in N.I.A. section 4-1 (b-f)).

The award of unemployment compensation pursuant to chapter 4 of the National Insurance Act follows procedural rules outlined in the Initiatives for Promoting Employment Act (I.P.E.A.) of 17 June 1947, No. 9, (N.I.A. section 4-8, also I.P.E.A. chapter V). The application for unemployment compensation is to be delivered to the Employment Office in the district where the applicant resides. The power of decision rests with the district's Employment and Measures Board, but in practice, it is the local Employment Office that reveiws the application and makes the decision pursuant to the authority delegated to it (I.P.E.A. section 29). Rejection of an application for unemployment compensation, or a decision to terminate unemployment compensation benefits can be appealed to the County Industry and Employment Board, and further appealed to the Directorate of Labour and finally to the Social Security Tribunal (I.P.E.A. section 30, paragraphs 2 and 3. Cf. Act on Appeal to the Social Security Tribunal of 16 December 1966, No. 9). According to a 1974 amendment to the Act, the Social Security Tribunal can no longer try the facts on which the administrative decision is based. Both the decisions of the Directorate of Labour and the Social Security Tribunal can be tested in the usual courts (I.P.E.A. section 30, paragraph 3); but in unemployment compensation cases, judicial control is not particularly practical.

The Basic Source and its Use
The Social Security Tribunal has since its establishment in 1967 and until 1983 rendered 43 judgments in cases in which women have appealed administrative decisions refusing or terminating unemployment compensation benefits. This is less than 12 percent of the total 354 judgments rendered relating to the rules for unemployment benefits. The percentage of cases appealed by women showed signs of increase towards the end of the 1970s in comparison to the percentage of cases appealed by men. However, after the change in the law on the rules of appeal

in 1974, the number of unemployment compensation cases overall declined sharply both in terms of absolute numbers and in
comparison to cases in other areas within the Social Security
Tribunal's jurisdiction. In addition, the substance of the judgments have changed character after this change in the law. They
have generally become shorter and more summary than before,
but this does not seem to apply to cases involving women as
much as to cases involving men. In order to gain a true impression of this national insurance scheme, there is need for
both legal and empirical studies covering the entire spectrum
of the labour market administrative agency decisions and routines at all levels. With these reservations in mind, the Social
Security Tribunal's judgments can be considered to be of special
interest as the authoritative source of the law in practice.

Starting with information about the extent and characteristics
of unemployment, rules on unemployment compensation, and
the decisions of the Social Security Tribunal, I shall describe
and evaluate women's right to unemployment compensation
from a practical point of view.

Even though the decisions of the Social Security Tribunal
only represent a small and probably a distorted sample of
conflicts in reality, these decisions will be used here to raise and
examine the problems indicated in this basic source as relevant
for women's law. The principal aim is thus not to analyze the
substance and limits of current law in general, e.g. by examining
statutory interpretation in the Social Security Tribunal's individual decisions. The principal aim is, through better insight into
practice, to trace the principles and to familiarize ourselves
with specific rules that seem to have a special significance for
women's practical reality, and to evaluate the unemployment
compensation system itself on the bases of the findings reached
through such a method of examination.

8.2. Definitions of Unemployment: The Scope of the Problem

'Registered unemployment'
Unemployment is a complicated concept, whose definition
varies with the purpose in mind. 'Registered total unemployment with the Employment Offices' is the official and most

often used definition, and it is used as the incidence of unemployment in the Directorate of Labour's statistics for the labour
market. The figure reflects persons who do not have income-
producing work, but who seek income-producing work, are able
to work and otherwise available for work. A person is considered to be registered with the Employment Office as seeking
employment if the person has registered or renewed a registration before the last whole calendar week prior to the day of
the unemployment count. The count is taken on the last work-
day of the month. Students who seek summer jobs are not
considered unemployed. Unemployment is stated in absolute
numbers or as a percentage of the labour force calculated from
the previous year by totalling the numbers of those having
employment and of the registered unemployed.

There are many temporary and more permanent unemployed
who have no reason to report to the Employment Office. This
Office's *job placement* comprises only about 25 percent of all
job placement in Norway. The majority of those who terminate
their jobs or begin to work after finishing school, seek and find
jobs independently of the Employment Office.

According to the Initiatives for Promoting Employment Act,
employers are, under threat of criminal punishment, required
to report all vacant jobs (I.P.E.A. section 12, cf. section 40). One
might therefore imagine that most people sought employment
through the Employment Offices because of their overview of
job possibilities. However, this duty to report is complied with
only to a small degree. The authorities have now and then
attempted without success to enforce it more stringently. Even
though organized private employment agencies are prohibited
(I.P.E.A. chapter IV), in practice employees and employers find
each other through private channels and the classified section
of newspapers. There are many indications that the best jobs
are not reported to the Employment Office, nor do those with
the best qualifications contact this Office. Its figures primarily
represent unemployed persons with relatively weak resources.

The criteria applied in the statistical compilations result in
the statistics principally accounting for those who have a legal
right to unemployment compensation. It is these who primarily
have reason to register with the Employment Office if the situation in the labour market is such that there are problems in

finding suitable work. Lacking employment, they thus have a right to society's alternative and second-best solution: money. Those who expect that the Employment Office will not have suitable work to offer and at the same time know that they do not satisfy the requirements for unemployment compensation, do not have sufficient incentive to register as unemployed, unless they know that they may be offered other types of services or support, such as various kinds of mobility-promoting aid. To what extent the Employment Office attracts the hidden unemployment with these special offers is dependent upon government policy at the time. At present young people especially, but also women and other specially targeted groups, are offered benefits of this type, primarily to cover the labour market's changing needs, but also to mitigate certain aspects of the unemployment situation.

Until the middle of the 1970s it was often said that there was 'full employment' in Norway. This meant that the annual average number of unemployed registered with the Employment Offices amounted to less than 1 percent of the labour force. Even during slow economic growth in the middle of the 1970s the unemployment percentage did not go much higher than this average. Unemployment of this size was not viewed as a problem of a social nature, but rather as a natural consequence of the labour market in motion (Foss 1980:22).

For women, however, registered unemployment was far greater, averaging over 2 percent in the 1970s. There are comparatively more women than men registered as unemployed, because women generally have a more tenuous connection to paid work than men. Women's percentage of registered unemployment has, moreover, climbed throughout the 1970s, both in relation to women's increasing percentage of the work force and in relation to men. After 1982 the rate of unemployment for men increased, but the percentage of unemployment for men is for all years lower than the percentage for women.

The tendency toward higher unemployment among women has not simply been a symptom of increased unemployment. It is also a result of women's increased participation in the marketplace and thus of the greater risk of unemployment among women, but also an indication of relative improvement from the point of view of women's independent economy. Married women accounted for most of the increase in the labour force during the 1970s, yet the demand for employment continues to be greater than the supply, just as women's first jobs in the marketplace are often insecure. It is only now that women have come into the marketplace on a large scale. Once they have come into it, they are, however, expelled much more easily than men. They have of course, like men, a right to unemployment compensation as a rule.

Also with respect to the requirements necessary to entitle one to receive and continue to receive unemployment compensation, women are generally in a weaker position than men. Family life, care work, and the lack of child care centres often make it difficult for women to be available for work to the extent required by the rules for unemployment compensation (Directorate of Labour 1982, Christensen 1979 and 1980 b, Petersen 1980).

Finally, unemployment compensation generally gives lower payments to women than to men, because the rules for compensation are connected to one's income before one becomes unemployed. The current rate of unemployment compensation measured per day now equals 0.002 of one's income during the last year of employment, or the average income of the three years immediately preceding unemployment. Add to this figure a supplement for the support of dependents and in some cases a supplement for other purposes fixed by law (N.I.A. section 4-3-5). Women's income in the marketplace is far below that of men, and there are many reasons for this. In the marketplace, education, career experience and seniority are important factors in the regulation of salaries.

The average differences in hourly pay between men and women office workers in Norwegian industry was 15.77 kroner or 33 percent in 1978. Control for career experience and seniority, and the difference decreases further. Control for all the factors that are disproportionately distributed between the sexes and which influence the regulation of salary, and the difference becomes 9.16 kroner, or almost 20 percent of men's hourly wage. This difference must presumably be attributed to unlawful sex discrimination (Titlestad 1983).

Even if we investigate differences in the levels of positions, or in job conditions, or different branches, the same pattern emerges: women have an average hourly wage lower than that of men. The difference evens out somewhat if one accounts for different sets of lawful salary criteria, but there always remains a certain amount unaccounted for—the tell-tale sign of sex discrimination (ibid: 108 f).

That women work less in the marketplace than men is reflected much more in the difference in income-level than in different kinds of job. Whereas it is usual for women to have part-time jobs, it is unusual for men. In the first quarter of 1978, 51 percent of all working women worked part-time, while only 5 percent of men had part-time jobs (Ellingsæter 1979). The total average working hours per week for all employed workers in 1978 was 29.1 hours for women and 40.4 hours for men. For the population as a whole, the average number of working hours per week was 13.8 hours for women and 21.6 for men (Ljones 1981:31,33). Whereas women in certain periods have unpaid care work and housework as their chief occupations and thus are totally absent from the marketplace without any salary or compensation other than maternity benefits, such a situation rarely applies to men.

All of these circumstances result in women's income being lower than men's, and as a consequence the average unemployment compensation paid to women is lower than that paid to men. When one takes into consideration the fact that unemployment compensation covers between 65–75 percent of one's net income, it means that unemployed women often have little to live on, even if they have a right to social security.

Several market forces that reduce women's salaries and social security arise from the particular conditions of the married woman's life. But these forces also have an impact upon young and unmarried women as a result of employers' presumptions that women will marry and become housewives, and upon solitary mothers (single mothers, divorcees, and widows). The latter group will more often than others be in the situation that unemployment compensation will not be sufficient to live on (Terum 1983).

'Job Seekers Without Income'
The expression 'job seekers without income' is used in the quarterly *Study of the Labour Force* (AKU) carried out by the

Central Bureau of Statistics. The study is based on interviews with a representative sample of the population between the ages of 16 and 74. The incidence of unemployment is the number of persons who answer 'yes' to the question whether they had tried to find income-producing work in the week prior to the date of the interview, such work either to have begun immediately or sometime during the week of the interview. The question is put to persons who in AKU's judgment are outside the labour force, i.e., to persons employed for less than one hour during the week of the interview and whose absence from the labour force is not merely temporary.

The criteria for being 'employed' in this sense are very broad, and the figures therefore cover a rather large area of under-employment. This under-employment especially concerns women, since it is women who have the majority of part-time jobs, and many of them desire more working hours if they could get them (Ellingsæter 1979). The AKU definition of those who are totally unemployed embraces more than the Directorate of Labour's statistics, and it is closer to the international require-ments demanded of employment-unemployment statistics estab-lished in the International Labour Organization's (ILO's) guide-lines. In the years 1978 and 1979 the unemployment according to AKU was approximately 60 percent higher than the figures of the Directorate of Labour, and on the average for the period between 1972–79 unemployment was under 2 percent of the labour force (Foss 1980:22).

'Potential Job Seekers'
The categories 'potential job seekers without income' and 'job seekers without income' give the best approximate picture of Norway's unemployment in fact. The first category includes persons outside the labour force who want income-producing work, but who for various reasons do not seek such work. Data on this group are routinely collected by the Central Bureau of Statistics, but are not published. Unemployment as defined by this category was examined closely by AKU in the fourth quar-ter of 1976. The question on desire for employment and reasons for not seeking employment when one desired it, was put to persons outside the labour force, i.e., to those who stated that they performed housework, went to school or otherwise pursued

studies, were without employment or busy with something other than income-producing work. The sick, disabled, retired and those doing military service were initially not taken into consideration. The figures for unemployment according to this method of calculation approximated 175,000, and over 100,000 of these were housewives, in addition to the proportion of women making up the other groups.

To get a total picture of under-employment among the sick, disabled and retired, additional questions were put to these groups. The unemployment figures rose by 44,000 (15,000 of these being disabled). Here too, housewives continued to comprise well over half of the total. The most usual reason stated for not seeking work, even though one desired it, was that there was no suitable work to be had. Travel to and from work and working hours were the two most dominant determinants of suitable work among the women interviewed. The women desired work in the town or community where they resided and they wanted part-time employment. Many also gave the lack of child care centres as the reason for not seeking work (Foss 1980:25-30).

The number of married women outside the labour force who desire work is considered to have been approximately 100,000 during the 1970s. In the same period there was a net increase of over 120,000 married women who entered the labour force.

We see how the percentage of female unemployment shows a significant increase the more one expands the groups of those defined as unemployed. The distortion revealed by the hidden figures behind the statistics for registered unemployed, is due, inter alia, to the formulation of the rules for unemployment compensation. Large groups of unemployed women do not register as unemployed with the Employment Office, because they do not fulfil the basic condition for the right to unemployment compensation, i.e., they have not earned the minimum income required. When at the same time they know that there is no suitable work to be had, they have also no economic reason to register as unemployed. The reasons stated for not seeking work even though one desires it also appear in the unemployment compensation scheme as a basis for rejection of an application for unemployment compensation from registered unemployed women. Women who have family and home responsibilities are not to the same extent as men, available for work, and therefore have greater problems than men in satisfying the requirements of (1) being unemployed through no fault of one's own, (2) being available for work, and (3) taking offers of employment which the Employment Office deems suitable. On the other hand, special consideration is given to unemployed mothers with young children with respect to the demand for geographical mobility: in this respect, unemployed men are subject to discrimination.

There is also a group of men who are registered as unemployed according to the Directorate of Labour's statistics, but who are not entitled to unemployed compensation because they do not satisfy the social security system's so-called eligibility requirement of an earned minimum income. It is primarily unemployed young people and social rejects who are in this position. Finally, there are groups of unemployed men who hide behind social programs other than the national insurance scheme for the unemployed. Sickness benefits, rehabilitation aid, disability pensions and early retirement of various kinds hide problems of under-employment among men. It is especially the rules on disability pensions which have provided a safety net for many long-term unemployed in the older age groups in districts with little industrial base (Kolberg 1976, Kjønstad (ed.) 1984).

8.3. The Requirement of Market-Connection

Even if the general requirement for membership in the national insurance scheme is fulfilled (cf. N.I.A. chapter 1), those seeking employment who have never had any connection with the marketplace because they come straight from school, have been in the home caring for children, or for other reasons have not been in the labour force, will have no right to unemployment compensation. This is a consequence of the social security system's eligibility requirements formulated in section 4-3-2, paragraph 6, of the National Insurance Act. The provision requires an earned minimum income of at least 75 percent of the National Insurance Act's 'basic amount' at the time the application for unemployment compensation is filed. As of 1 March 1985, that would mean NOK 16,350 (the basic amount is generally NOK 21,800).

The earned income must be earned within the last completed calendar year before the application for unemployment compensation is filed. Those seeking employment who have earlier connections to the marketplace thus lose their rights during an absence from the marketplace of a certain duration.

The requirement of a minimum earned income must be presumed to be absolute. Among the decisions of the Social Security Tribunal there is only one case concerning this question. The case involved a woman who for 14 years had been employed as a part-time cleaner, and who had in all of those years paid social security tax according to the Act on Social Security Against Unemployment of 1959, which applied before the scheme for unemployment benefits was incorporated into the National Insurance Act in 1970. According to the rules of 1970, which were not related to the 'basic amount', but required a minimum earned income of NOK 4000, she did not fulfil the requirement, since she had only earned NOK 3714. The Social Security Tribunal found that neither the text of the law, the legislative history, nor any other source of law could support any interpretation other than a rejection of her claim (A 1208/71). There is no reason to believe that 'minimum earned income' eligibility requirement would not be just as strictly construed today, even though the calculation method has changed.

The delimitation of persons eligible for social security, a consequence of the requirement of a connection to the marketplace, affects women to a significant degree. The first delimitation, which affects newcomers to the market, affects also many men. But the effect of this is mitigated by the rule that the King can prescribe rules that put compulsory national service on an equal footing with work in the service of others (N.I.A. section 4-3-4 (d)). Such a regulation was enacted by a Royal Decree of 25 May 1973. Compulsory national service is understood to mean not only compulsory military service, but also service in the home guard (reserves), civilian service for conscientious objectors, and service in the civil defence. The Ministry of Local Government and Labour, or any person to whom it delegates authority, can establish more detailed rules relating to this practice. Compulsory national service's equal status with income-producing work is today valued at three times the 'basic amount', i.e., an annual salary of NOK 65,400. ('Regulations of Unemployment Compensation to Members Who Have Served Compulsory National Service', established by the Ministry of Labour on 13 November 1978). The eligibility requirement would be fulfilled after 3 months service, which is thus the minimum for coming under the social security's scheme for the unemployed.

This special rule was brought about by an amendment of 13 April 1973, No. 19, without the bill receiving any special attention or express justification (Ot.prp. No. 27 (1972–73)). But it was obvious that the reason for the amendment was that persons in career-active ages were over long periods kept away from salaried work because of a service made compulsory by society (NOU 1983:19 page 17). This compulsory national service gave no right to unemployment compensation (cf. section 4-2-3 (f)), and only to a minor extent a right to financial indemnification, which was not looked upon as salary in relation to the rules on unemployment compensation. It was therefore considered reasonable that society should assist in this way if the person doing compuslory national service found himself without a job at the end of his service.

The amendment applies only to those who have a duty of service and consequently not to women who elect to serve in these capacities, nor does it apply to the few women who perform civil defence service, since they usually would not satisfy the three-month service rule.

This line of reasoning is not used to place women's socially necessary task of child-bearing and child-rearing on an equal footing with income-producing work with respect to unemployment benefits. It is the official position that there is no legally-enforceable duty to give birth to children. But in my opinion, policy considerations ought to dictate the equating of child-bearing and child-rearing with compulsory national service.

The rights of women without a connection to the marketplace are also weak when the social security rules for maternity benefits are concerned. Such women only have a right to maternity benefits in the form of a small lump-sum allowance established by Parliament (N.I.A. section 3-21-6, NOK 3654 as of 1 January 1985). Women working in the marketplace are paid maternity benefits for up to 90 days from the time they stop working (N.I.A. section 3-21-2). Moreover, many women take advantage of their legal right to extended leave of absence without salary during the child's first year, cf. Working Environment Act section 31, item 3. This legally permitted absence has no protection from loss of rights with respect to the eligibility for unemployment compensation rules (N.I.A. section 4-3-2, paragraph 6, cf. paragraph 1).

In addition, women, to a larger extent than men who perform compulsory national service, will often lose their previously earned rights because of the interruption caused by care work. Compulsory national service does not last so long that the rights earned in the preceding three years' average income are significantly affected by the period of compulsory national service. The insured may choose the three-year average as the basis of calculation if the result is better than when only the special rule for compulsory national service is used as a basis of calculation. Interruptions for women caused by care work will often last much longer, as regards both care of one's own children and of elderly and sick relatives. The situation is thus not only that such child-bearing and care work do not give independent rights; women also lose rights earned from previous work in the marketplace, since periods of childbirth and care work are not protected from the loss of rights with respect to the 3-year rule in N.I.A. section 4-3-2, paragraph 6.

Although it is the minimum requirement for unemployment benefits which is discussed here, it can be mentioned that the same circumstances that significantly affect the satisfying of the eligibility rules also determine the size of the social security benefit. Nor are paid maternity benefits taken into account i.e., treated as income in the calculation of the unemployment compensation's base figure, such as is the case with paid sickness benefits (N.I.A. section 4-3-2, paragraph 2, does not treat maternity benefits on a par with sickness benefits), and paid-out unemployment compensation, as decided by the King under the authority granted him (N.I.A. section 4-3-4 (f)).

A woman who terminates income-producing work in order to give birth to a child loses previously earned rights with respect to unemployment benefits if she becomes unemployed shortly after she returns to work, even if she limits her absence to the period of time prescribed by the Working Environment Act.

There has been a certain amount of discussion about this situation recently. Parliament's Standing Committee on Local Government and employee organizations have expressed a need for studies on the extent to which 'other activity' ought to be treated as income-producing work (see statements in connection with other amendments, Inst. O.No. 14 (1977–78):3; Inst. O.No. 24 (1979–80):3).

In Report to the Storting No. 14 (1977–78) 'On the Politics of Employment', the Government announced the appointment of a committee to examine the question whether the right to unemployment compensation should rest on some other basis than previous earned income. The persons in mind were those doing unpaid care work in the home as their chief occupation, and those who after the completion of their education cannot find suitable work. The committee was appointed in January 1978 and delivered its report in December 1982 (NOU 1983:19 Unemployment Compensation – Care Work and Education).

The report recognizes in principle the need for both rules providing alternative bases for earning rights to unemployment compensation and rules that protect the loss of previously earned rights, so-called 'transition rules'. Care work for the elderly and handicapped is highest on the list, and it is recommended that in certain situations care work should be treated as income-producing work—but with a valuation that corresponds only to the 'basic amount' and special supplement, which is far below what young boys receive for performing compulsory national service. For care of one's own children, no independent accrual of rights was proposed. On the other hand, such rights were proposed for completed years of education beyond the 7th grade, at the same valuation proposed for care of the elderly and handicapped. Moreover, certain types of 'transition rules' were proposed for periods of care of one's own children, as well as for care of the elderly and handicapped, and for certain periods of completed education. But the rules are still formulated in such a way that child care would continue to have an extremely weak position with respect to unemployment compensation if the proposals should be realized.

8.4. Basic Requirements for Unemployment Compensation

When an insured person loses income-producing work and seeks a new job, certain basic requirements must be fulfilled if that person is to be entitled to unemployment compensation until suitable work is found. She must be able to work (able-bodied), unemployed through no fault of her own, available for work and registered with the Employment Office in accordance with established rules (N.I.A. section 4-2-1).

These conditions must continue to be fulfilled throughout the period of unemployment if the person in question is not to lose her right to unemployment compensation. The National Insurance Act lists a number of special reasons for the exclusion from, or termination of unemployment compensation (section 4-2-3 (a–k)), several of which can be said to provide insight into the actual meaning of the basic requirements.

The requirement that one is to be 'able to work' means, inter alia, that the person in question does not receive sickness benefits, maternity benefits, or a disability pension, nor shall she be admitted to an institution of health (cf. section 4-2-3 (k and g)). Otherwise this requirement has little independent significance beyond the requirement that one is available for work.

The requirement that one be 'unemployed through no fault of one's own' means that one must be without income and objectively viewed as unemployed within the meaning of the law. The requirement also contains a disqualifying rule of fault. If the person in question has other income, for example from wages, private work, old age pension etc., one normally has no right to unemployment compensation. The same is true for persons admitted to and provided for in public institutions and persons performing compulsory national service (cf. section 4-2-3 (e–j)). The rule of fault must be viewed in connection with section 4-2-3, paragraph 4, which refers to section 4-2-3 (b–e), which specifies a long series of circumstances which the law characterizes as 'one's own fault'. Examples of this are when the insured has become unemployed because: (1) of reprehensible conduct; (2) she has resigned from previous employment that the Employment Office deems suitable for her; (3) she refuses to participate in training, re-education or rehabilitation programs offered by various government labour market agencies; or (4) she neglects to take part in readily available work in the service of others or for herself. In these cases the insured person is not only excluded from a right to unemployment compensation from the time the excluding act took place, but can also be excluded from unemployment compensation for a specific period of time (section 4-2-3, paragraph 4).

Similarly, the requirement that one is 'available for work' must be seen in connection with section 4-2-3 (c), refusal of an offer of suitable employment, which is the combination that most often occurs in cases before the Social Security Tribunal.

The requirement of section 4-2-1 and the reasons for exclusion or termination of section 4-2-3 are often not clearly distinguished in many judgments of the Social Security Tribunal, which in turn can lead one to talk in terms of basic requirements and continued requirements rather than basic requirements and reasons for termination. It is not the case that section 4-2-1 is only used in cases involving a person's right to receive unemployment compensation, while section 4-2-3 is used to terminate the right to unemployment compensation already granted. Section 4-2-1 is *also* used in connection with the termination of unemployment compensation payments, and it often seems arbitrary which reasons are stated in the decisions in individual cases. The same type of factual situations will in some cases be related to section 4-2-1 and in other cases to section 4-2-3, and there is the same type of interchange with respect to references to sub-sections within section 4-2-1, namely section 4-2-1 (b) and (c).

The requirements for receiving and continuing to receive unemployment compensation have not changed over time. The principles in today's legislation were established at the turn of the century in social security's private predecessor, the trade union's unemployment benefits' funds. The principles were codified in the obligatory unemployment benefits scheme introduced in the Act on Insurance Against Unemployment of 24 June 1938, No. 8, carried over into the Act on Insurance Against Unemployment of 28 May, 1959, No. 4, and were integrated into the National Insurance Act on 19 June 1970, No. 67 (see Dahl 1983 for a more detailed description of this development).

Because the requirements are the same, and the discretionary authority so broad that the lines separating the individual requirements are to a large extent unclear or non-existing, the legal issues raised under both the 1959 Act and the National Insurance Act (1970) are in the following treated as one.

'Able to work'
Those who are totally or partly occupationally disabled are as a rule entitled to sickness benefits, rehabilitation aid or a disability pension. The line separating these social security schemes and social security's unemployment scheme is adjustable, both in the individual case and in the collective swing of the market force's demand for labour. At times and places where the demand for labour is small, experience shows that consumption of the various social security benefits is influenced accordingly. Poor physical or mental health can lead to an employee dropping out of work for shorter or longer periods, and that can in some cases lead to confusion as to what kind of social security arrangement one is covered by. Nevertheless, the various benefits are coordinated in such a way that the receipt of sickness benefits, disability pensions, etc. excludes any right to unemployment compensation (section 4-2-2 (a) cf. section 4-2-3 (k and g)).

In the Social Security Tribunal appeals examined, there were no women who alleged their own poor health as a reason for restricting their availability for work. Nor were there any rejections of any applications for unemployment compensation based on section 4-2-1 (a). On the other hand, the rule in section 4-2-1 (a) has been examined in cases that men have appealed. That this has not occurred in cases appealed by women perhaps means that there must be more incentive for women to hang on to unemployment compensation if they have poor health in relation to the labour market. Housework is a good reason for women not to work, while more is required before men allow themselves (or can allow themselves) to be defined outside the marketplace.

'Unemployed Through No Fault of One's Own'
In order to receive unemployment benefits the applicant must be unemployed through no fault of her own. This means that

there must be reasonable grounds for one's unemployment. The most usual grounds recognized are termination because of the closing down of a company or the curtailment of operations, or unemployment in connection with temporary lay-offs. A person whose conduct has been reprehensible in connection with the loss of employment, or who has quit the job without reasonable grounds, will not be entitled to unemployment benefits.

The principal rule is that the cause of unemployment must be found in the work situation or market situation. Family reasons are not reasonable grounds for termination of one's employment. A woman who quits her job in connection with marriage in order to live with her husband will not be entitled to unemployment compensation if she finds herself unemployed in her new location, nor will a married woman who moves with her husband and children to the husband's new place of work. Such generally accepted social reasons for termination of employment are thus not 'reasonable' according to the rules for unemployment benefits, as they are at present enforced. The Social Security Tribunal puts it like this:

> ... there is of course no reason to blame Mrs. 'X' nor can it be considered unreasonable that she for the above-mentioned reasons moved from.... On the contrary this was the natural thing that most people in a similar situation would have done. But with respect to the rules for unemployment benefits, the decisive point is that she willingly chose to resign her position without there being any circumstances in her work giving rise to this. The reasons were purely private and personal, namely her marriage, and it is not the duty of the social security unemployment scheme to pay unemployment compensation for unemployment due to such reasons (A 59/67).

The rules on what kinds of work one can *resign* are more stringent than those on what kinds of work an unemployed person is required to take. An employee is not entitled to unemployment compensation if she resigns her job, even though it is located in such a place or is of such a nature that she could have refused to take such work if offered it while unemployed. What is considered 'suitable work' is evaluated differently, depending upon whether it is related to the rules for resignation of employment in section 4-2-1 (b) and section 4-2-3 (b), or to the rules for availability for employment in section 4-2-1 (c), cf. section 4-2-3 (c) (see below). A married woman with three children between the ages of 8 and 11 years resigned her job and moved with her husband to a new location where he began a new job; she was not entitled to unemployment compensation, even though as an unemployed person she could have refused to accept work outside the local market (A 4/70, see also A 2223/74: resignation of employment because of a salary offer below standard).

It is a general rule that 'with respect to the question of unemployment compensation, a person has a duty within reason to keep the job [she] has' until she has managed to obtain a new job (A 579/81: Disagreement at the workplace, see also A 996/72: poor lodging conditions at the workplace, A 334/69: poor working conditions, because of planned change in owner- ship and warning of dismissals from the employer).

A person can also *lose* a granted right to unemployment compensation because her conduct does not satisfy the require- ment of being unemployed through no fault of her own. To satisfy this requirement the person must be actively seeking employment and show a positive attitude to the work offered her, so that a new work contract can be concluded. By showing a negative attitude or scepticism toward the conditions of em- ployment, she can be deemed to be unemployed through her own fault. A woman seeking employment who stated that her work with four young children at home prevented her from reacting quickly enough to job offers was judged by the Social Security Tribunal to have 'reacted negatively' and therefore was not entitled to unemployment compensation (A 259/70, see also Christensen 1980 a:395 f).

'Available for Work'

In the majority of appellate cases where women have been denied unemployment compensation, the reason for the denial is that the applicant is not perceived as 'available for work', i.e., that she is not fully accessible to work in the marketplace. This is also a usual reason for unemployment compensation payments being terminated.

The requirement that one be fully available for work is closely connected to certain reasons for exclusion from and termination of unemployment compensation and especially to the unemployed person's refusal to take employment offered which the Employment Office deems suitable for her.

Prior statements of one's limited availability with respect to the nature of work or place of work, the number of working hours or time of day or night, can lead to the applicant being perceived as not fully available for work. 'The insured must be willing to take the type of work that the Employment Office deems suitable on the basis of the individual's talents and qualifications. Furthermore, one must in general be available for the entire labour market, i.e., that [she] must be willing to accept suitable work offered her, also outside [her] place of residence and usual career' (A 898/73). One, who 'makes such specific demands with respect to workplace, work duties, salary, working hours etc. that the possibility of the offer of suitable work is unreasonably reduced, cannot be considered fully available for work' (A 956/77).

The requirement of being fully available for work and the requirement of being willing to take suitable employment offered can have unclear lines of separation. In some cases the women had already at the time of application limited their availability so that their applications were rejected. In other cases unemployment benefits were terminated because the women refused suitable employment and therefore were not recognized as available for work. The law referred to seems to be somewhat arbitrary; several judgments referred to section 4-2-1 (c)—the requirement of being available for work—even though it was a matter of terminating unemployment benefits, in which case it perhaps would have been more appropriate to refer to section 4-2-3 (c).

In what ways do unemployed women limit their availability for work? In almost all the cases where the question of being available for work or the question of the limits of suitable employment arises, it is a matter of family considerations conflicting with the rules for unemployment benefits. Family considerations play a significant role in limiting the availability for work, particularly with respect to the work place (e.g. questions of moving, daily or weekly commuting, travel distance and means of transportation) and the working hours (e.g. desire for part-time work, shift-work, etc.). Difficulty with child-care service also occurs, but not so often as one might expect on the basis of the Danish and Swedish experience (Petersen 1980, Christensen 1980 b).

(a) The Right to 'Seek Only Local Employment'
To be available for work, the main rule is that the person seeking unemployment benefit must be available for the entire country's labour market, regardless of marital status and other family circumstances. 'I am married here' is a statement that indicates that one is not available for work (A 29/68).

Certain family and personal circumstances can, however, be taken into consideration and provide a right to seek only local employment. Those over 64 years old seeking employment have such a legal right. (Regulation of 14 February 1973 on The Relaxation of The Requirement of Availability for Work With Application for Unemployment Compensation from Unemployed Persons over 64 Years Old, established by authority of N.I.A. section 4-2-4, last paragraph). Other than this rule for the aged there exist no regulations or departmental circulars concerning the criteria for the right to seek only local employment, nor a more precise definition of the meaning of the concept. But one article in *Sosial Trygd* 1956 from the Directorate of Labour's Office of Social Security—at least in 1983—continued to be in use as a guide for case workers at local Employment Offices and in the Directorate of Labour. It states:

One cannot accept as a reasonable ground for an applicant's refusal to take work outside his place of residence or his natural work district, the claim of having to be at home because of work on his small farm, or only because he had to carry water or procure fuel etc. Nor is sickness an acceptable reason unless it concerns a serious sickness in the applicant's immediate family. With regard to women with young children, however, one cannot usually expect that such women will take work at a place farther away than they can live at home and, without great inconvenience, travel to and from work each day'. (*Sosial Trygd,* No. 1, 1956).

These guidelines are also applied and quoted by the Social
Security Tribunal (A 330/69) and have gradually developed into
a comprehensive and clear practice. The care of one's own
young children and of seriously ill members of one's immediate
family is accepted in some situations, but not always, as reasonable grounds for limiting the insured's geographic mobility.
Those permitted to seek only local employment are allowed to
live where they reside and to seek a job to which they can travel
there and back each day without great inconvenience.

Women with young children are the most unproblematic examples. They are, without further question, permitted to seek only
local employment; the practice has a long tradition behind it.
There was some controversy over the scope of this exception in
the 1950's during the drafting of the Act on Insurance Against
Unemployment of 1959. One faction of the Judicial Committee
was suspicious of the free practice that had developed, while another faction of equal strength wanted to make it even more free,
so that all married women would have a general right to seek only
local employment, regardless of whether there were children in
the family. The Ministry and Parliament supported the middle
position, which was applied in daily practice—that it is women
with infant children who are entitled to seek only local employment (see Dahl 1983 for more detail).

The limit for what is normally understood as 'young' is also
rather flexible. It appears that 'children' up to 18 years of age
are given weight; at least they are of importance if there are
several children in the family.

Married women without children or with grown children at
home must be available for the entire nation's labour market.
Exceptions are made only if there is serious sickness in the
immediate family, or in the case of advanced age. A sick spouse
does not give a woman the right to seek only local employment
if the sickness is not serious. *Angina Pectoris* was found not to
be sufficiently serious to give the spouse a right to seek only
local employment. The sick person must require daily care, and
a medical certificate that the spouse's presence is necessary must
be submitted (A 1280/78).

The applicant's advanced age can also relieve her of the duty
to move her residence. As previously mentioned, persons of 64
years of age or more have a legal right to seek only local

employment, but in individual cases, discretion can lead to a younger person being granted a similar right. Nevertheless, a married woman of 55 years of age who for many years had worked in the local dairy was dismissed when the dairy was closed down. Her unemployment compensation was terminated because she refused to move from her house, husband, and elderly mother (A 617/70).

It is only mothers with the responsibility for young children who benefit from the child-care rule, not older sisters (A 643/70: young girl with partially disabled mother, unwell father, and younger sisters and brothers of compulsory school age). Nor do fathers benefit, if they are not sole supporters. The Social Security Tribunal has rejected appeals from many fathers, regardless of the number of children and the degree of the wife's sickness. The practice is strict, and discriminatory against fathers and husbands with respect to their possibility to fulfil family responsibilities. Both the Children's Act and the Spouses Property Relationship Act impose upon men duties of care for family and household which the enforcement of unemployment compensation rules most probably prohibits them from fulfilling.

(b) Part-time Work and Shift-Work
Part-time work is a woman phenomenon. Of 439,000 part-time workers (35 hours or less per week) in 1975, 380,000 or 87 percent were women. Of all employed persons between the ages of 16 and 74 in the first quarter of 1978, 51 percent of the women and only 5 percent of the men were part-time workers. If we take into consideration the fact that these statistics also include retired males, it would appear that among men in career-active ages the percentage of part-time workers is even lower (Ellingsæter 1979).

The increasing use of part-time workers in society raises several problems with respect to unemployment benefits. The principal rule is that the person seeking employment, in order to receive unemployment benefits, must be available for full-time employment. She must also accept shift-work within reason. The point of departure is thus that one cannot receive unemployment compensation if one restricts one's availability with respect to the number of working hours and time of day or night, and that unemployment compensation payments will be terminated if the insured, on the basis of working hours, refuses to take employment offered which the Employment Office deems suitable. In such a situation the insured would not satisfy the requirement of being available for work.

The question of part-time work is closely related to the question of the right to seek only local employment both in fact and in law—in fact, in that the women who want part-time work almost always also request the right to seek only local employment; in law, in that the same kinds of factors and themes come up for discretionary judgement in both instances. The right to limit one's availability with respect to working hours is, however, a more recent phenomenon than the right to limit one's geographic mobility. For a long time seekers of part-time employment were completely excluded from unemployment benefits. Even if they had for many years worked in a part-time job and paid social security tax just as other employees, they acquired no rights.

In 1965 the Directorate of Labour changed the practice. Part-time employees were in principle to be treated just like other employees, if they had an 'acceptable reason' for demanding part-time work. The guiding rule for an 'acceptable reason' was that 'the applicant couldn't, or only with great difficulties could, work a full-time job, for example, because of poor health, care of young children etc.'. It was emphasized that one had to be 'very strict' in one's evaluation (Departmental Circular No. 18/65/05 of 25 June 1965 on Unemployment Compensation to Persons Who Cannot Work Full-Time). The Social Security Tribunal has approved these guidelines in several decisions (A 344/68, A 1526/81, A 898/73).

What does it mean to be strict in one's evaluation? Although it is sufficient for a woman to have young children in order to have the right to seek only local employment, in order to be entitled to seek only part-time work it is additionally required that the children are so young that they need supervision during normal working hours and that the mother cannot, or only with great difficulty can, manage to get someone to care for the children. A mother with young children thus cannot choose whether to combine supervision of the children and work by taking part-time work; she is required to utilize available nurseries or baby/child sitters and to take full-time employment.

While older children (not yet 18 years of age) can form the basis of a mother's right to seek only local employment – in any case if there are several of them—this is not the case with respect to the right to seek limited working hours. A woman who was 'willing to accept a job several hours a day, e.g. as a cleaner', and who asserted that she had a husband and two sons to care for, was not entitled to seek only part-time work (A 898/73. The sons were, however, declared to be adults without any ages being mentioned in the case). Nor was a woman with an availability of approximately 3 hours per day acceptable, on the grounds that her child was 17 years old and the mother therefore was not required to restrict her availability (A 1526/81).

The sickness of a spouse is, however, an acceptable reason. Such a sickness is required to be documented by a medical certificate to the effect that 'the applicant is needed at home due to the sickness of her husband' (A 344/68). A woman whose husband had a 100 percent disability pension and a daughter 17 years old had her unemployment compensation terminated because she refused to take full-time work, but the decision was overruled on appeal to the Social Security Tribunal (A 648/78).

In connection with the submission of the medical certificate, the social security administrative authorities have the duty to inform and actively investigate the substance of the claims. A woman who requested evening shift-work, on the basis that her disabled husband ought not be alone at home all day was refused unemployment compensation because her husband's disability was lacking proper documentation with respect to the need for care. The Social Security Tribunal discussed the decision, stating that the social security administrative authorities themselves should have investigated the case (935/78, also see A 649/69).

The overruled cases from the end of the 1970s can indicate that the Social Security Tribunal is in the process of softening up the rules for part-time work. It is, however, too early to tell whether the tendency will last.

Even if the job seeker is granted the right to limit her working hours, the limitations must be 'reasonable with respect to how short a time and when in the day or night the person wants to work'. A person who wants to work less than the average one-third of the trade's normal working hours per week, cannot as a rule be said to be available for work, entitling one to unemployment compensation. The same applies to a person requesting work at such hours of the day or night that 'the Employment Office has no reasonable possibility to place the individual'. What an insured person can request will thus be dependent upon the circumstances of the local labour market. Such unusual cases of limited availability must have extraordinary justification if unemployment compensation is to be granted (Department Circular No. 18/65/05).

It is a different matter when the job seeker is available for normal full-time work, but is offered shift-work in whole or in part outside normal working hours, or part-time work despite the wish for full-time work. In such situations, can she have reasonable grounds for refusing an offer of employment that is otherwise considered suitable?

A woman, with four children under 18 years of age and a weekly commuting husband, was offered shift-work at a military mess hall for English officers. She refused the job, complaining of its inconvenient working hours (evening shift) and the lack of public transportation home. Referring to the fact that someone would drive her home, she pointed out that it was difficult for her to entrust herself to irregular rides from foreign officers, since she lived alone with children and was an outsider, having recently moved to the rural district. Moreover she claimed that she was completely unaccustomed to the kind of work that was offered (serving among other things at cocktail-parties), and that she completely lacked the courage necessary to take on such a job. The Social Security Tribunal found that this was suitable work (A 1545/78). In my opinion the borderline for what is suitable work was clearly exceeded in this case.

A divorced mother with a son 14 years of age was offered employment at a guest house located within the geographical area normally accepted for persons seeking only local employment. Part of the work consisted of an evening shift, and on those days the insured could not come home at night because there was no public transportation at that time of night. The Social Security Tribunal found (despite dissent) that the working hours were not suitable for a single mother with a child of school age (A 330/69).

A usually full-time worker who is offered part-time work is required to take it. On the other hand, she has a right to 'reduced aid' as compensation for the unwillingly imposed reduction in working hours and income (regulations established by Royal Decree of 1 October 1976 on Unemployment Compensation for Persons With Reduced Working Hours and Income).

Reduced unemployment compensation is paid to insured persons who receive less income because of a reduction in working hours, and to the partially unemployed who cannot find full-time employment (A 336/79, A 262/70).

The practice seems to be that the insured must accept part-time work even if her total situation of work and income is significantly worse than it was previously. The insured has a duty to change careers, and in questions concerning the job offered versus the previous job, there is a tendency to evaluate each factor separately without the total work situation of the employment offered being seen in relationship to the total work situation of the previous employment. How much worse the employment offered is permitted to be has, as far as I know, never been taken up for discussion by the Social Security Tribunal, at any rate, not in the cases where women are the appellants.

'Reduced aid' is to compensate for the reduction of the usual weekly working hours. But the aid is not paid if the reduction of working hours is less than 20 percent. Usual working hours for full-time work are calculated according to the employment contract which applied prior to the reduction of working hours, but not beyond the number of working hours permitted by law for the trade or profession in question. For insured persons who have not had fixed working hours and for unemployed persons who take part-time employment, the Directorate of Labour can promulgate detailed regulations regarding what is to be meant by 'usual working hours'.

Large groups of those receiving reduced aid (for example laid-off workers) have entered into contracts in which reduced working hours were imposed by the employer. Less clear is the answer to the question what is to be meant by the expression 'usual working hours' if the insured has had a marginal or changing relationship to the labour market, which is often the case with women. This can involve the situation where: (1)

the employment contract only states a minimum or maximum number of working hours; (2) a totally unemployed person has previously worked full-time, but thereafter had shorter working hours and/or more sporadic employment than before becoming unemployed; (3) the person worked part-time before her working hours were reduced; and (4) the person who has worked irregular hours over shorter periods of time, for example, temporary work or work of unspecified duration.

Earlier, the desired working hours of these groups were often used as the basis of their 'usual working hours', since it was not of their own accord that they worked part-time or worked under uncertain employment contracts. However, the regulations were made more stringent on 1 November 1981, because they in some cases led to payments that could be perceived as a form of subsidization, which was not the intention of the social security system.

The group 'usual working hours' is now established according to the average number of working hours during the four calendar weeks immediately preceding the filing of the application for unemployment compensation, or according to the average number of working hours during the last 12 months if this produces a significantly better result for the applicant. This means that a number of persons have had their unemployment compensation terminated on the basis of the new rules for determining 'usual working hours'.

8.5. Conclusion

The negative discrimination against unemployed women is breached at one point only: on the question of the right to seek only local employment. Here women have a right deriving from their function as carers that men are not granted even if they so request.

Apart from that, the different treatment on the basis of sex is systematic, indicating that unemployment among women and unemployment among men are by far two different social realities, with respect to the incidence, the characteristics, and the causes of unemployment. Yet the rules of law pertaining to unemployment are gender-neutral.

This discrepancy between a gender-specific reality and a gender-neutral body of law leads in practice to the same rules having different effects and different significances for the two sexes. A right granted in a rule fashioned from a life situation typical for men can result in women falling outside the application of the rule or occupying a weak position within the application of the rule. It is the rule's criteria (typical for men) for the granting of the right which places women in this weak position.

In order to redress women's weaker position in law generally, gender-specific rules have been used, for example, the mother's previous priority in child custody cases, or the Working Environment Act's rules for special protection for women in certain situations. This way of creating a 'just distribution' has been used throughout this century, but is now on the way out of legal politics, being replaced by neutral rules suitable to both sexes.

In order to redress these inequalities with respect to unemployment benefits, one must no doubt resort to rules common to both women and men, but rules that in reality guarantee women a stronger position in the scheme of unemployment compensation that social security offers to people who can't earn a living.

One can start with the moral and political duty derived from Article 110 of the Constitution. When a person who has performed care work at home over a period and to an extent generally considered useful and necessary for society registers as unemployed without being able to find suitable work, does not society have a duty to aid this person, to the same extent that it aids employees with paid work when they are in need of new employment?

If the answer is 'yes', one is, in my opinion, bound to take one of the following three paths:

If care work in the home were to provide greater rights and these rights were to include a salary for caring, some of the problems I have discussed in this chapter would be resolved. Women would then receive an income for care work, and this income would be used as the basis of calculation for the social security system's eligibility requirement and for the measurement of unemployment compensation. A salary for caring would of course be gender-neutral and be given to the person in the family who takes this work as opposed to work outside the home.

Another approach is to eliminate the eligibility requirement for unemployment benefits. Today's eligibility requirement rests on the unemployed's previous income: the fact that a person has had income-producing employment in the private or public sphere qualifies her for unemployment compensation. With the elimination of the eligibility requirement, one would have to give a minimum social security to all who registered with the Employment Office as unemployed. Those who had not previously performed paid work could, if so decided, be required to fulfil a longer qualificatory period before the right to unemployment compensation became operative.

A third approach would be to strive for a guaranteed minimum income for all adults. The State would thus provide a means of support to a reasonable degree, whether she or he was employed or unemployed, and whether the work was traditional paid work or care work.

In all seriousness none of the three approaches I have outlined are utopian—not even the most comprehensive proposal for a guaranteed minimum income for everyone. Many tendencies in our society today lean in the same direction, both in the private and in the public sector. The institutional structures of work together with its basic values steadily strive for greater forms of guarantees: guaranteed workplaces, safety for local society, rights with respect to dismissal, and protection of the individual's rights to security. In the public sector workers enjoy a much higher degree of protection, while at the same time more and more of what this sector actually deals with consists of redistributing means to safeguard industries, jobs and structures that we wish to preserve. Not to mention the entire social security system, which today in practice weaves the safety net rather tightly under each and every one of us. The road toward a guaranteed minimum income for everyone in this respect can represent a common road, and is simpler to construct in comparison with the rather complicated question of rights that the entire network of social security benefits and the public sector as a whole represents.

Whether utopia or reality, today's inequalities in the social security system's treatment of unpaid care work and paid work is in the long run obviously untenable. That the inequalities of today's social reality systematically affect men and women differently makes it all the more debatable.

References

Aarbakke, Magnus 1965. 'Kutymen som rettskilde' (Business Customs as Sources of Law). *Tidsskrift for Rettsvitenskap* pp. 432 f. Oslo.

Aarbakke, Magnus 1966. 'Harmonisering av rettskilder' (Harmonizing the Sources of Law). *Tidsskrift for Rettsvitenskap* pp. 499 f.

Andenæs, Johs. & Helge Kvamme 1969. 'Om grunner til uenighet om rettsspørsmål' (Reasons for Legal Disputes). *Nordisk Gjenklang. Festskrift til Arnholm*, Oslo: Tanum.

Anners, Erik 1983. *Den europeiske rettens historie* (History of European Law). Oslo: Universitetsforlaget.

Atkins, Susan & Brenda Hoggett 1984. *Women and the Law*. Oxford: Blackwell.

Aubert, L. M. B. 1887. *Den norske Privatrets almindelige Del. Første Afdeling* (Norwegian Private Law. Part One). Kristiania.

Aubert, Vilhelm, Torstein Eckhoff & Knut Sveri 1952. *En lov i søkelyset* (Searchlight on a Law). Oslo: Akademisk Forlag.

Augdahl, Per 1973. *Rettskilder* (Legal Sources). Oslo: Aschehoug.

Benum, Inga Nakling 1976. *Om hjelpestønad og forhøyet hjelpestønad til funksjonshemmede barn og ungdom. En undersøkelse foretatt i Troms 1975* (Benefit and Supplementary Benefit to Handicapped Children. A Survey Conducted in Troms, Norway, 1975). Universitet i Tromsø.

Berge, Astrid Schlytter 1982. 'Jämställdhetslagen' (The Equal Opportunity Act). *Årbog for Kvinderet*, Copenhagen: Juristforbundets Forlag.

Bjørnsen, Torill 1979. 'Kvinner og uføretrygd' (Women and the Disability Pension). *Hefte for kritisk juss* Nos. 3/4. Oslo.

Boe, Erik 1979. *Distriktenes utbyggingsfond* (The Norwegian Regional Development Bank). Oslo: Universitetsforlaget.

Boe, Erik 1985. *Styring og støttemuligheter.* (Directing or Supporting the Regions). Oslo: Universitetsforlaget.

Bratholm, Anders & Nils K. Sundby (eds.) 1976. *Kritisk juss* (Critical Legal Studies). Oslo: Pax Forlag.

Bruun, Niklas 1982. 'Finsk jämställdhetslagstiftning i stöpsleven' (The Making of the Finnish Equal Opportunity Act) *Årbog for Kvinderet*. Copenhagen: Juristforbundets Forlag.

Bull, Kirsti Strøm 1979. 'Avtaler mellom ugifte samboende' (Agreements between Unmarried Couples). *Tidsskrift for Rettsvitenskap* 1979 pp. 82 f.

Bull, Kirsti Strøm 1982. 'Hjemmearbeidets erstatningsrettslige stilling' (The Status of Housework in Tort Law). *Tidsskrift for Rettsvitenskap* pp. 903 f.

Bull, Kirsti Strøm 1983. 'Ugift samliv—noen synspunkter på rettsutviklingen i Sverige og Norge' (Unmarried Couples and Their Legal Positions in Sweden and Norway). *Tidsskrift for Rettsvitenskap* pp. 590 f.

Callemann, Catharina et al. 1984. *Kvinnoreformer på männens villkor* (Women's Reforms on Men's Conditions). Lund: Studentlitteratur.

Castberg, Frede 1975. 'Fra naturrett til "kritisk juss"' (From Natural Law to Critical Legal Theory). *Jussens Venner*. Oslo.

Christensen, Anna 1980 (a). *Avstängning från arbetslöshetsersättningen* (Exclusion from Unemployment Benefits). Stockholm: Norstedt.

Christensen, Anna 1980 (b). 'Barntillsyn och arbetslöshetsersättning' (Child Care and Unemployment Benefits). *Årbog for Kvinderet*. Copenhagen: Juristforbundets Forlag.

Christensen, Anna 1984. 'Två syn på rättsvätenskapen' (Two Perspectives of Legal Science). *Hefte for kritisk juss* No. 3/4. Oslo.

Christensen, Bent 1980. *Forvaltningsret. Hjemmelsspørgsmål* (Public Administration Law. Legal Foundations). Copenhagen: Juristforbundets Forlag.

Criminal Law Advisory Council Report on Pornography and Punishment, 1985.

Dahl, Tove Stang 1976. 'Ekteskapet, den moderne husmannskontrakten' (Marriage as the Modern Crofter's Contract). Stören & Wetlesen (eds.) *Kvinnekunnskap*. Oslo: Gyldendal.

Dahl, Tove Stang 1980 (a). 'Tre stikkord om barns rettsstilling' (Three Keywords re the Legal Position of Children). A. Bratholm (ed.). *Barnerett Institutt for kriminologi og strafferetts stensilserie* No. 35. Universitetet i Oslo.

Dahl, Tove Stang 1983 (a). 'Forholdet mellom individuelle motiver og kollektive interesser i sosialpolitikken' (Individual Motives and Collective Interests in Social Politics). *Nordisk Sosialt Arbeid* pp. 3 ff.

Dahl, Tove Stang 1983 (b). *Fordeling og styring gjennom arbeidsløshetstrygden* (Unemployment Benefits: Distributive vs. Directive Aspects) Mimeo. University of Oslo: Institute of Public Law.

Dahl, Tove Stang 1984. 'Da JURK ble til' (The Birth of JURK). *Hefte for kritisk juss* No. 3/4.

Dahl, Tove Stang (ed.) 1985. *Kvinnerett I-II* (Women's Law I-II). Oslo: Universitetsforlaget.

Dahl, Tove Stang, Kjersti Graver, Anne Hellum & Anne Robberstad 1976. 'Likhet og urett' (Equality and Injustice). Bratholm & Sundbye (eds.) *Kritisk juss*, Oslo: Pax Forlag.

Dahlberg, Anita 1980. 'Jämställdheten—förtryck eller gynnande?' (Equal Opportunity: Repression or Advantage?). *Årbog for kvinderet* Copenhagen: Juristforbundets Forlag.

Dahlberg, Anita 1981. 'Kvinnorätt från Stockholms horisont' (Women's Law as seen from Stockholm). *Årbog for kvinderet,* Copenhagen: Juristforbundets Forlag.

Dahlberg, Anita 1984. *Jämt eller i bland—Om jämställdhet* (Always or Sometimes—On Equality). Stockholm: Arbeitslivscentrum.

Dalla Costa, Mariarose 1972. *Potere femminile e soverzione sociale* (Women's Power and Social Oppression). Padova: Marsilio Editore.

Eckhoff, Torstein 1971 (a). *Rettskildelære* (Sources of Law). Oslo: Tanum.

Eckhoff, Torstein 1971 (b). *Rettferdighet ved utveksling og fordeling av goder* (Justice in the Exchange and Distribution of Benefits). Oslo: Universitetsforlaget.

Eckhoff, Torstein 1984. 'Hva rettsvitenskapen er og hvad den bør være' (What Legal Science Is and What It Should Be). *Hefte for kritisk juss* No. 3/4.

Edelberg, Einar 1979. 'Ligebehandlingsloven' (The Equal Opportunity Act). *Årbog for kvinderet.* Copenhagen: Juristforbundets Forlag.

Ellingsæter, Anne Lise 1979. *Deltidsundersøkelsen* (Investigation into Part-Time Work). Rapport. Oslo: Statistisk Sentralbyrå.

Elster, Jon 1985. *Self-Realization in Work and Politics*, Paper prepared for the conference on 'Marxism and Democracy', University of Chicago March 1985.

Eriksson, Lars D. 1984. *Medborgarnes likställinghetsprincip och positiv särbehandling* (The Principle of Equal Rights as against Positive Discrimination). Paper delivered at the Nordic Symposion for Equal Opportunities, Helsingfors Sept. 1984.

Eriksson, Lars D. 1985. 'Rätten och juristerna i framtiden. Visioner och utopier' (Law and the Lawyers in the Future. Visions and Utopias) *Retfærd* No. 28.

Fastvold, Marianne 1977. 'Fødselsrett og likhet' (Birth Law and Equality). *Kvinnerettslige studier* No. 2. Universitetet i Oslo.

Fastvold, Marianne 1985 (a). 'Rettssikkerhet under fødsel' (Legal Rights during Childbirth). T. S. Dahl (ed.) *Kvinnerett* II. Oslo: Universitetsforlaget.

Fastvold, Marianne 1985 (b). 'Kvinners arbeid og integritet i familien' (Married Women's Work and Integrity). In T. S. Dahl, (ed.) *Kvinnerett II*, Oslo: Universitetsforlaget.

Fastvold, Marianne & Anne Hellum 1985. 'Vi har prøvd å la kvinnene komme til orde. Teori, kilder og metode' (An Attempt to let the Women speak for themselves. Theory, Sources and Methods). A Project Report from University of Oslo: Institute of Women's Law.

Firestone, Sulamith 1970. *The Dialectics of Sex*. New York: William Morrow.

Fodstad, Hjørdis & Karen Sophie Steen 1977. 'Det skjulte martyrium. Omkring synliggjøring av brutalitet i hjemmet' (The Secret Martyrdom: Family Violence Revealed). *Institutt for kriminologi og strafferetts stensilserie* No. 26. Oslo University.

Føllesdal, Dagfinn, Lars Walløe & Jon Elster 1983. *Argumentasjon, språk og vitenskapsfilosofi* (Arguments, Language and the Philisophy of Science). Oslo: Universitetsforlaget.

Foss, Olav 1980. *Holdninger og atferd på arbeidsmarkedet* (Opinions and Behaviour in the Labour Market). Rapport. Oslo: Statistisk Sentralbyrå.

Gjelsvik, Astrid & Elisabeth Dons Wankel 1980. 'Gjenlevende ektefeller og andre enker' (Surviving Spouses and other Widows), *Kvinnerettslige studier* No. 11. Universitetet i Oslo.

Gjeldsvik, Nikolaus 1912/1968. *Innledning til retsstudiet* (Introduction to the Law Course). 5th Edition, Oslo.

Gulli, Brita 1980. 'Abortlovgivningens historie' (History of the Anti-Abortion Laws) in Gotaas et al. *Det kriminelle kjønn* (The Criminal Sex). Oslo: Pax Forlag.

Hagerup, Francis 1888. 'Nogle Ord om den nyere Retsvidenskabs Karakter' (Some Remarks on the Nature of Recent Jurisprudence). *Tidsskrift for Retsvidenskab* pp. 2 f.

Halvorsen, Marit 1985 (a). 'Diskriminering ved ansettelser. Om likestillingslovens §4, 2. ledd' (Discrimination in Appointments: section 4, paragraph 2 of the Norwegian Equal Opportunity Act). In T. S. Dahl (ed.) 1985.

Halvorsen, Marit 1985 (b). 'Juridisk rådgivning for kvinner—en fortelling fra virkeligheten' (Women's Legal Counselling—a true Fairy Tale). *Retfærd* No. 28. Copenhagen.

Haukaa, Runa 1977. 'Kommentar til begrepet kvinnekultur' (A Note on the Concept of Women's Culture). In A. M. Berg et al. *I kvinners bilde*. Oslo: Pax Forlag.

Hellum, Anne 1985. 'Penger og verdighet etter ektefellelovens § 1' (Money and Dignity: The Norwegian Act on Property Relationship between Spouses section 1). In T. S. Dahl, (ed). 1985.

Hellum, Anne, Marianne Kjøllesdal & Annie Krefting 1979. 'Omfordeling eller forfordeling gjennom skattereglene. En kvinnerettslig interesseanalyse' (Redistribution or Discrimination in Taxation Rules). *Kvinnerettslige studier* No. 5. Universitetet i Oslo.

Hernes, Helga Maria 1982 (a). *Staten—kvinner ingen adgang* (The State—No Entrance for Women). Oslo: Universitetsforlaget.

Hernes, Helga Maria 1982 (b). 'Offentliggjøring av familien' (The Family goes Public). In Haukaa et al. (eds.) *Kvinneforskning: Bidrag til samfunnsteori.* Oslo: Universitetsforlaget.

Høigård, Cecilie & Annika Snare 1983. *Kvinners skyld* (Women's Guilt). Oslo: Pax Forlag.

Hoel, Marit 1982. 'Kvinnefellesskap og arbeiderfellesskap i industribedrifter— to sider av samme sak?' (Women's and Workers' Industrial Communities: Two Aspects of One Issue?). In Holter (ed.) *Kvinner i fellsskap.* Oslo: Universitetsforlaget.

Holgersen, Gudrun 1984. *Likestillingsloven* (The Norwegian Equal Opportunity Act). Bergen: Universitetsforlaget.

Holter, Harriet 1977. 'Kvinneforskning: Historisk utvikling og aktuelle motsetninger' (Women's Studies: Their History and Recent Contradictions). In Berg et al. *I kvinners bilde.* Oslo: Pax Forlag.

Jacobsson, Ulla 1982. 'Processrätt och kvinnorätt' (Procedural Law and Women's Law). *Institutt for offentlig retts skriftserie* No. 3. Oslo: Universitetsforlaget.

Jaggar, Alison et al. 1983. *Feminist Politics and Human Nature.* Sussex: The Harvester Press.

Ketscher, Kirsten 1984. 'Legalstrategier i kvinderetten' (Legal Strategies in Women's Law). *Hefte for kritisk juss* Nos. 3–4. Oslo.

Kjønstad, Asbjørn 1978. 'En sammenlikning mellom trygderettslige forarbeider og lovforarbeider fra den "sentrale jus"' (Social Security Laws vs. 'Basic' Laws: A Comparison of their Legislative Histories). *Lov og Rett* pp. 3 f. Oslo.

Kjønstad, Asbjørn 1980. 'Pengekrav' (Money Claims). *Tidsskrift for Rettsvitenskap* pp. 528 f. Oslo.

Kjønstad, Asbjørn 1984 (a). 'Verdsetting av tapt arbeidsevne, særlig til å utføre husarbeid' (Evaluating the Value of Work, particularly Housework). *Tidsskrift for Rettsvitenskap* pp. 335 f.

Kjønstad, Asbjørn 1984 (b). 'Husmorsameiet og rettsutviklingen' (The Housewife's Rights in Current Jurisprudence). *Tidsskrift for Rettsvitenskap* pp. 554 f.

Kjønstad, Asbjørn (ed.) 1984. *Folketrygden i støpeskjeen* (Changing Prospects for the Social Insurance System). Oslo: Universitetsforlaget.

Kolberg, Jon Eivind 1976. *Hvorfor kommer så mange på trygd, og flere enn forventet?* (Why so Many on Social Security, and More than Expected?) Mimeo, Universitetet i Tromsø.

Krüger, Kai 1978. *Pengekrav* (Money Claims). Bergen: Universitetsforlaget.

Kvam, Grete 1977. 'Stønad til enslige forsørgere' (Sole Provider Benefits). *Institutt for offentlig retts stensilserie* No. 18. Universitetet i Oslo.

Ljones, Olav 1981. 'Arbeidstidsproblemer' (Problems of Working Hours). In Brunstad et al. *Sysselsettingen i søkelyset.* Bergen: Universitetsforlaget.

Lykkjen, Asti Magni 1976. *Voldtekt* (Rape). Oslo: Pax Forlag.

Martinsen, Kari & Kari Wærness 1979. *Pleie uten omsorg.* (Nursing without Care). Oslo: Pax Forlag.

Mathiesen, Thomas 1971. *Det uferdige* (The Unfinished). Oslo: Pax Forlag.

Melby, Kari 1980. 'Prostitusjon og kontroll' (Prostitution and Control) In Gotaas et al. *Det kriminelle kjøn,* Oslo: Pax Forlag.

Nielsen, Ruth 1981. *Individual Justice and/or Women's Integration into Working Life.* Copenhagen: Women's Research Centre in Social Science.

Nielsen, Ruth & Jytte Thorbek 1979. *Ligestillingslovgivning* (Legislation on Equal Opportunities). Copenhagen: Juristforbundets Forlag.

NOU 1976:12. *Familiebeskatning* (Government White Paper on Family Taxation).

NOU 1979:38. *Om tilleggspensjon og sykepenger til omsorgspersoner* (Government White Paper on Pensions and Sickness Benefits to Caring Persons).

NOU 1981:16. *Reklame og kjønn* (Government White Paper on Gender and Advertizing).

NOU 1983:19. *Dagpenger under arbeidsløyse—omsorgsarbeid og utdanning* (Government White Paper on Unemployment Compensation, Caring Labour and Education).

Øie, Ole-Erik 1976. 'Trygderetten og dens virksomhet' (The Social Security Tribunal and its Functions). *Institutt for offentlig retts stensilserie* No. 11. Universitetet i Oslo.

Øyen, Else, (ed.) 1981. *Garantert minsteinntekt i Norge* (Guaranteed Minimum Income in Norway). Bergen: Universitetsforlaget.

Olsnes, Ragnhild 1985. 'Retten til sjølvbestemt abort' (The Right to Self-determined Abortion). In T. S. Dahl (ed.) 1985.

Peterson, Bente 1980. 'Børnepasning set i relation til arbejdsløshedsforsikring' (Child Care and Unemployment Benefits). *Årbog for Kvinderet* Copenhagen: Juristforbundets Forlag.

Piven, Francis Fox 1985. 'Women and the State: Ideology, Power and the Welfare State' in A. Rossi (ed.) *Gender and the Life.* New York: Aldine.

Platou, Oscar 1915. *Forelæsninger over Retskildernes Theori* (Lectures on the Theories of Legal Sources). Kristiania: T. O. Brøgger.

Posner, Richard 1977. *Law and Economics.* Little Brown & Co.

Rasmussen, Nell et al. 1982. *Voldtegt—på vej mod en helhedsforståelse.* (Rape: Towards an Understanding of its Complexity). Copenhagen: Delta.

Rawls, John 1983. *A Theory of Justice.* Oxford University Press.

Rødseth, Tor & Kristin Dale Titlestad 1984. *Kvinner i arbeid. Økonomiske og sosiale perspektiver* (Women in Work: Economic and Social Perspectives). Oslo: Universitetsforlaget.

Rognlien, Knut 1977. *Særskilt ligning av bondekoner* (Separate Taxation of Farmers' Wives). Thesis for law degree. Universitetet i Oslo.

Ross, Alf 1953. *Om Ret og Retfærdighed* (On Law and Justice). Copenhagen.

Ross, Alf 1963. 'Naturret contra retspositivisme' (Natural Law vs. Positive Law). *Tidsskrift for Rettsvitenskap* pp. 479 f. Oslo.

Sætness, Ingvil 1977. 'Intensjon og virkelighet. En undersøkelse av søknader til hjelpestønad og forhøyet hjelpestønad' (Intentions and Realities: An Enquiry into the Requests for Benefit and Supplementary Benefit). *Sosial Trygd* No. 3. Oslo.

Sandvik, Gudmund 1984. 'Schweigaard'. *Jussens Venner* No. 8. Oslo.

Seip, Jens Arup 1984. 'Rettsstaten—en studie i begrepsanalyse og begrepsforvirring' (The Rechtsstaat: A Study in Conceptual Analysis and Confusions). *Nytt Norsk Tidsskrift* No. 2. Oslo.

Skirbekk, Gunnar 1985. 'Schweigaard og den norske tankeløysa' (Schweigaard and the Norwegian Thoughtlessness). *Jussens Venner* No. 8. Oslo.

Skjeie, Hege 1982. *Den som lo først, LO best* (The Norwegian TUC and the Equal Opportunity Act). Diploma in political science. Universitetet i Oslo.

Skjeie, Hege 1985. *Fortrinnsrett—ingen forpliktelse* (Advantage, but no Obligation). Mimeo. Oslo: Institutt for Samfunnsforskning.

Smith, Carsten 1980. *Bankrett og statsstyre* (Banking and Government). Oslo: Universitetsforlaget.

Smith, Eivind 1979. *Forvaltningsrett og blandingsadministrasjon* (Administrative Law in a Government of Mixed Administration). Oslo: Tanum.

Smith, Lucy 1975. 'Kvinnerett—mål og midler' (Women's Law—Means and Ways). *Institutt for privatretts stensilserie* No. 30. Universitetet i Oslo.

Smith, Lucy 1980. *Foreldremyndighet og barnerett* (Child Custody and Children's Rights). Oslo: Universitetsforlaget.

Sørensen, Bjørg Aase 1977. 'Arbeiderkvinner og Verdighet' (Working Women and Dignity). In Anne Marie Berg (ed.) *I kvinners bilde. Bidrag til en kvinnesosiologi.* Pax, Oslo.

Stang, Fredrik 1933. 'Om Rettsvidenskap. Et tilbakeblikk' (A Hindsight on Legal Science). *Tidsskrift for Rettsvitenskap* pp. 118 f. Oslo.

Straffelovrådet 1985. Innstilling om pornografi og straff (Criminal Law Advisory Council: On Pornography and Punishment). Oslo.

Sundby, Nils Kristian 1974. 'Positivistisk og kritisk juss' (Positive and Critical Jurisprudence). *Samtiden* No. 6. Oslo.

Sverdrup, Tone 1981. 'Mellom ekteskapskontrakt og lønnskontrakt' (Between Marriage Contract and Wage Contract). *Institutt for offentlig retts skriftserie* No. 5. Universitetet i Oslo.

Sverdrup, Tone 1982. 'Mellom ekteskapskontrakt og lønnskontrakt' (Between Marriage Contract and Wage Contract). *Institutt for offentlig retts skriftserie* No. 3. Oslo: Universitetsforlaget.

Sverdrup, Tone 1984 (a). 'Lovvern for arbeidstakere i andres hjem' (Legal Protections of Employees in Other Persons' Homes). *Kvinnerettslige Arbeidsnotater* No. 31. Universitetet i Oslo.

Sverdrup, Tone 1984 (b). 'Folketrygden i kvinneperspektiv' (Social Security from Women's Perspective). In A. Kjønstad (ed.) 1984.

Sverdrup, Tone 1985. 'Det to-sporede lovsystemet—belyst med eksempler fra skatteretten' (The Two-Track Legal System in the Light of Tax Law Issues). In T. S. Dahl (ed.) 1985.

Terum, Lars Inge 1983. *Sosialhjelp. Ei analyse av sosialutgifter og sosialhjelpsmottakarar* (Social Benefits: An Analysis of Expenses and Clients). INAS Report No. 2. Oslo.

Thue, Helge Johan 1983. *Samliv og sameie* (Cohabition and co-ownership). Oslo: Tanum-Norli.

Titlestad, Kristin Dale 1983. 'Timelønnsforsjeller mellom kvinner og menn'

(Wage Differences between Women and Men). In I. Blom et al. *Kjønnsroller og likestilling*. Bergen: Universitetsforlaget.

Unger, Roberto M. 1986. *The Critical Legal Studies Movement*. Harvard University Press.

Vestergaard, Emma 1974. 'Om voldtægtsofre. Victimologi' (The Victimology of Raped Women). *Nordisk Tidsskrift for Kriminalvidenskab* pp. 151 f. Copenhagen.

Vogt, Agnes 1981. 'Kvinners rett til fellesboligen ved separasjon og skilsmisse' (The Rights of Separated and Divorced Women). *Institutt for offentlig retts skriftserie* No. 2. Oslo: Universitetsforlaget.

Wærness, Kari 1979. 'Kvinner og trygd' (Women in the Social Security System). In J. E. Kolberg and K. Wærness (eds.) *Trygd og samfunn*. Oslo: Universitetsforlaget.

Wærness, Kari 1982. *Kvinneperspektiv på sosialpolitikken* (Social Politics in Women's Perspective). Oslo: Universitetsforlaget.

Wahl, Anna & Herman Bohne 1973. *Forhøyet hjelpestønad* (Supplementary Benefits). Tønsberg: Fylkeslegen i Vestfold.

Westerhäll-Gisselsson, Lotta 1979. *Kvinnor och rätt* (Women and Law). Stockholm: Liber Förlag.

Widerberg, Karin 1980. *Kvinnor, klasser och lager* (Women, Classes and the Laws). Stockholm: Liber Förlag.

Widerberg, Karin 1984. 'Världens bästa reformer? Den svenska foräldraledighetslagstiftningen och verkligheten' (World's Best Reforms? The Reality behind the Swedish Rules of Parents' Leave of Absence during Children's Sickness). *Jussens Venner* Nos. 6–7. Oslo.

Index